THE TWELVE POWERS

Also by Charles and Cora Fillmore

TEACH US TO PRAY

Also by Charles Fillmore

ATOM-SMASHING POWER OF MIND
THE CHARLES FILLMORE CONCORDANCE
CHRISTIAN HEALING
DYNAMICS FOR LIVING
JESUS CHRIST HEALS
KEEP A TRUE LENT
METAPHYSICAL BIBLE DICTIONARY
MYSTERIES OF GENESIS
MYSTERIES OF JOHN
PROSPERITY
THE REVEALING WORD
TALKS ON TRUTH

THE TWELVE POWERS

CHARLES AND CORA FILLMORE

Unity Classic Library

Unity Village, MO 64065-0001

First combined edition 1999; fourth printing 2005;
ninth soft cover printing 2011

The Twelve Powers is a member of the Unity Classic Library.

The Unity Classic Library is guided by the belief of Unity cofounder Charles Fillmore that "whatever God has revealed to man in one age He will continue to reveal to him in all ages." The series projects Fillmore's vision of Unity as "a link in the great educational movement inaugurated by Jesus Christ" to help and teach humankind to use and prove eternal Truth.

To place an order, call the Customer Service Department: 1-800-669-0282 or go online at *www.unitybooks.org*. For information, address Unity Books, 1901 NW Blue Parkway, Unity Village, MO 64065-0001.

Cover design by Gretchen West

Library of Congress Cataloging-in-Publication Data

Fillmore, Charles, 1854–1948.
    [Twelve powers of man]
    The twelve powers / Charles and Cora Fillmore.
        p.   cm. — (Unity classic library)
    Includes texts of: The twelve powers of man, by Charles
    Fillmore; Christ enthroned in man, by Cora Fillmore.
    ISBN 0-87159-311-4
    ISBN 978-0-87159-311-5
    1. Unity School of Christianity—Doctrines. I. Fillmore,
    Cora. Christ enthroned in man. II. Title. III. Series.
    BX9890.U505F58 1999
    289.9'7—dc21   98-33330
                                                         CIP

Canada BN 13252 9033 RT

Editor's Note

Early writings on the twelve powers go back to the work of New Thought pioneers Emma Curtis Hopkins and Annie Rix Militz in the late nineteenth century. Charles and Myrtle Fillmore, Unity's cofounders, were part of a group of metaphysicians who experimented with and discussed these ideas.

Charles wrote early articles about inner power, and his book *Christian Healing* (1909) discusses some of these powers, although his ideas were not yet fully formed. On April 24, 1912, he published in *Weekly Unity* the introduction of what was to become his book *The Twelve Powers of Man*. This introduction proved popular and was reprinted several times. In 1920 Charles published the series "The Twelve Powers of Man," and it was reprinted in 1925–26 and 1929–30 in *Unity Magazine.*

Cora Fillmore, who became Charles' second wife in 1933 after Myrtle's passing in 1931, published a series of articles entitled "Following Jesus in the Regeneration" in 1925–26 that was printed in conjunction with the reprint of the twelve power series. In 1929–30 both Charles' and Cora's series were reprinted. Her essays were revised and expanded and their names changed to become a "Drill for the

Development of. . ." whatever specific power was being highlighted.

When Charles Fillmore's *The Twelve Powers of Man* was published in 1930, it did not include any of Cora's material; twenty-three printings followed. In 1937, Cora's essays were bound together to form *Christ Enthroned in Man.*

The Twelve Powers brings together for the first time in book form the twelve power teachings of Charles and Cora Fillmore that were originally published in *Unity Magazine.* We are indebted to researcher and writer Neal Vahle, author of *Torch-Bearer to Light the Way: The Life of Myrtle Fillmore,* for the original information that the Fillmore essays had been published together. We also are grateful to Carolyn Stewart and Eric Page of the Unity Archives for doing the research that provided us with most of the above information.

We presented the idea of publishing as part of the Classic Library series a new edition that included both Charles' and Cora's work. This idea was approved by both Charles R. Fillmore and Connie Fillmore Bazzy. We kept the format you see in this book to protect the integrity of *The Charles Fillmore Concordance;* it has not been affected by this change.

We have attempted to preserve the historical integrity of the original Fillmore writings as much as possible. Bracketed clarification of archaic or unclear words has been added; and corrections have been made only of obvious errors that otherwise would result in serious confusion in punctuation, capitalization, spelling, and syntax. The Fillmores' use of uppercase pronouns referring to Jesus Christ has been retained, but it should be noted that the modern style is to lowercase the pronouns to suggest the humanity rather than the deification of Jesus.

Furthermore, we would like the reader new to Unity to understand that not all Charles Fillmore's assertions regarding regeneration, physical immortality, and sexuality are universally accepted among Unity people today. Out of historical accuracy, we have presented the material as Charles published it. However, one of the great strengths of the Unity movement, which Charles himself heralded, if not pioneered, was the right of each individual to make up his or her own mind. Here the reader is invited to do just that.

It is our sincerest hope that this new edition, which provides the opportunity for reading Charles' more theoretical essays along with Cora's more practical applications, will help clarify these core teachings of Unity.

—Michael A. Maday
1998

"Regeneration is not possible without love. . . . There must always be continuous constructive action between the masculine and feminine faculties of soul and body; but the anointing with the precious love of the divine feminine is necessary to the great demonstration."

Charles Fillmore

Cora Fillmore

Table of Contents

Book One

The Twelve Powers of Man

Book Two

Christ Enthroned in Man

Book One

THE TWELVE POWERS OF MAN

by
Charles Fillmore

Introduction

J esus prophesied the advent of a race of men who would sit with Him on twelve thrones, judging the twelve tribes of Israel. This book explains the meaning of this mystical reference, what and where the twelve thrones are, and what attainments are necessary by man before he can follow Jesus in this phase of his regeneration. Regeneration follows generation in the development of man. Generation sustains and perpetuates the human; regeneration unfolds and glorifies the divine.

It is not expected that beginners in the study of metaphysical Christianity will understand this book. It deals with forces that function below and above the field of the conscious mind. The average religious thinker knows nothing about the subconscious mind and very little about the superconscious; this book presupposes a working knowledge of both.

This book aims to clear up the mystery that ever envelops the advent, life, and death of Jesus. To the superficial reader of the Gospels His life was a tragedy and, so far as concerns the kingly reign that was prophesied, it was a failure. Yet those who understand the subtlety of the soul and supremacy of Spirit see that Jesus was conqueror of a psychic force that was destroying the human race.

Jesus was the star actor in the greatest drama ever played on earth. This drama was developed in the celestial realm, its object being to inject new life into

3

perishing men. The full significance of this great plan of salvation cannot be understood by man until he awakens faculties that relate him to the earth beneath and the heavens above.

It had long been prophesied that the time was ripe for the advent on this planet of a new race, and there had been much speculation as to the character and advent of the superman. Herein is set forth the metaphysical idea of the spiritual quickening of man on the human plane and his transformation into the divine: not by a miracle or the fiat of God, but by the gradual refinement of the man of flesh into the man of Spirit. As Paul taught, "This corruptible must put on incorruption, and this mortal must put on immortality."

Jesus was the "first-fruits" of those who are coming out of the mortal into the immortal. He was the type man, the Way-Shower, and, through following His example and taking on His character as a spiritual-minded man, we shall come into the same consciousness.

Spiritual discernment always precedes demonstration; consequently, more is taught in this book as a possibility of attainment by man than has been demonstrated by any man save Jesus. Those who feel that they are ready for the great adventure in the attainment of eternal life in the body here and now should not be deterred because there are no outstanding examples of men who have risen to this most exalted degree. Through mental energy, or the dynamic power of the mind, man can release the life of the electrons secreted in the atoms that compose the cells of his body. Physical science says that if the electronic energy stored in a single drop of water were suddenly released, its power would demolish a six-story building. Who can estimate the power stored in the millions of cells that compose the human body? The method of release of this body energy and its control are mystically taught by Jesus. He was transfigured before His apostles, "and his face did shine as the sun, and his garments became white as the light." Before His crucifixion He had attained such mastery over His body cells that He told the Jews that they might destroy His body and "in three days" He would "raise it up." He demonstrated this in the resurrection of His body after it had been pronounced lifeless. When He disappeared in a cloud He simply unloosed the dynamic atoms of His whole body and released their electrical energy. This threw Him into the fourth dimension of substance, which He called the "kingdom of the heavens."

The dynamic energy that man releases through prayer, meditation, and the higher activities of his mind is very great, and if not controlled and raised to the spiritual plane, may prove a source of body destruction; if carried to the extreme, it may even prove a cause of soul destruction. "Be not afraid of them that kill the body, but are not able to kill the soul: but rather fear him who is able to destroy both soul and body in hell." This one who is able to destroy both soul and body in Gehenna is the personal self or selfish ego that is in man.

The electronic energy in man is a form of fire, which is represented by Gehenna. This electronic fire must be used unselfishly. If used to further the selfishness of man it becomes destructive, through the crosscurrents that it sets up in the nervous system.

We do not encourage those who still have worldly ambitions to take up the development of the twelve powers of man. You will be disappointed if you seek to use these superpowers to gain money (turn stones into bread), control others ("the kingdoms of the world . . . All these things will I give thee"), or make a display of your power ("If thou art the Son of God, cast thyself down"). As recorded in the fourth chapter of Matthew, these are the temptations of the selfish ego which Jesus had to overcome and which all who follow Him "in the regeneration" have to overcome.

Unspeakable joy, glory, and eternal life are promised to those who with unselfish devotion strive to develop the Son of God consciousness. All the glories of the natural man are as nothing compared with the development of the spiritual man. The things of this world pass away, but the things of Spirit endure forever. In his flesh body, man may be compared to the caterpillar that is the embryo of the butterfly. In its undeveloped state the caterpillar is a mere worm of the earth, but it has, infolded within it, a beautiful creature awaiting release from its material envelope. Paul visualized this when he wrote in Romans 8:22: "For we know that the whole creation groaneth and travaileth in pain together until now. And not only so, but ourselves also, who have the first-fruits of the Spirit, even we ourselves groan within ourselves, waiting for *our* adoption, . . . the redemption of our body."

Jesus, the Great Teacher, gave many lessons for our instruction, the greatest and most mystical being The Revelation of John. Here He showed Himself to John as He is in His redeemed body. He stood in the midst of seven lights, which represent the seven ideas of Divine Mind ruling in the restored earth. "One like unto a son of man, clothed with a garment down to the foot, and girt about at the breasts with a golden girdle. And his head and his hair were white as white wool, *white* as snow; and his eyes were as a flame of fire; and his feet like unto burnished brass, as if it had been refined in a furnace; and his voice as the voice of many waters. And he had in his right hand seven stars: and out of his mouth proceeded a sharp two-edged sword: and his countenance was as the sun shineth in his strength."

This description of the appearance of Jesus is partly symbolical, because John did not himself understand the full import of the powers that were being exercised by the spiritual man, whose words were so clean-cut that they appeared to John as a two-edged sword, whose eyes were so discerning that they seemed a flame of fire, whose voice was like the rippling of many waters. Language is poor and bare when one seeks to describe the glories of the spiritual state. Comparisons within the comprehension of the reader are necessary, and they but tamely tell of the superhuman man and his powers.

However, this pen picture by John of what he saw when he was lifted up "in the Spirit on the Lord's day" gives us a glimpse of what the redeemed man is like, and what we shall attain when we "awake, with thy likeness."

It should be thoroughly understood that this sight of Jesus that was given to John was not a vision of a man who had died and gone to heaven up in the skies, but it was the opening of John's eyes to existence in what may be termed the fourth-dimension man. We use this term *fourth dimension* because it is the name given to a state of existence that popular material science says must be, in order to account for the effects that are being expressed on every side. It is also called the interpenetrating ether, which is not to be understood as something material, or as being matter, but as something having properties far more substantial than matter. Through the application of mathematical principles, scientific men are proving the existence of the spiritual side of Being. This does not refer to the psychical realm in which undeveloped souls rest while awaiting reincarnation. Many people take it for granted that soul realms and spiritual realms are identical. But these stand to each other as moonshine and sunshine. Jesus called the interpenetrating state of being the kingdom of heaven, or, in the original Greek, "the kingdom of the heavens." He said that it was like a treasure hid in a field, which, when a man discovered it, he would sell all that he had to buy. The majority of Christians believe that they are going to this heaven when they die, but Jesus does not teach that the dead go first to glory. On the contrary, Jesus teaches that death may be overcome "If a man keep my word he shall never see death." Paul taught that Jesus attained victory over death. "Christ being raised from the dead dieth no more . . . . Let not sin therefore reign in your mortal body, that ye should obey the lusts thereof: neither present your members unto sin *as* instruments of unrighteousness; but present yourselves unto God, as alive from the dead, and your members *as* instruments of righteousness unto God."

The Psalmist writes:
"What is man, that thou art mindful of him?
And the son of man, that thou visitest him?
For thou hast made him but little lower than God,
And crownest him with glory and honor.
Thou makest him to have dominion over the
works of thy hands;
Thou hast put all things under his feet."

With the mind of the seer, Ralph Waldo Emerson says:
"Great hearts send forth steadily the secret forces that incessantly draw great events, and wherever the mind of man goes, nature will accompany him, no matter what the path."

"Verily I say unto you, that ye who have followed me, in the regeneration when the Son of man shall sit on the throne of his glory, ye also shall sit upon twelve thrones, judging the twelve tribes of Israel. And every one that hath left houses, or brethren, or sisters, or father, or mother, or children, or lands, for my name's sake, shall receive a hundredfold, and shall inherit eternal life."

—Jesus Christ
(Matthew 19:28–29)

CHAPTER 1

The Twelve Powers of Man

THE SUBCONSCIOUS realm in man has twelve great centers of action, with twelve presiding egos or identities. When Jesus had attained a certain soul development, He called His twelve apostles to Him. This means that when man is developing out of mere personal consciousness into spiritual consciousness, he begins to train deeper and larger powers; he sends his thought down into the inner centers of his organism, and through his word quickens them to life. Where before his powers have worked in the personal, now they begin to expand and work in the universal. This is the first and the second coming of Christ, spoken of in the Scriptures. The first coming is the receiving of Truth into the conscious mind, and the Second Coming is the awakening and the regeneration of the subconscious mind through the superconscious or Christ Mind.

Man expands and grows under divine evolution as an industrial plant grows. As the business expands, it is found that a system is necessary. Instead of one man's being able to do the work with the assistance of a few helpers, he requires many helpers. Instead of a few helpers, he needs hundreds; and in order to promote efficiency he must have heads for the various departments of the work. Scripture symbology calls the heads of departments in man's consciousness the Twelve Apostles.

Each of these twelve department heads has control of a certain function in soul or body. Each of these heads works through an aggregation of cells that physiology calls a "ganglionic center." Jesus, the I AM or central entity, has His throne in the top head, where phrenology locates spirituality. This is the mountain where He so often went to pray. The following outline gives a list of the Twelve, the faculties that they represent, and the nerve centers at which they preside:

Faith——Peter——center of brain.
Strength——Andrew——loins.
Discrimination or Judgment——James, son of Zebedee——pit of stomach.
Love——John——back of heart.
Power——Philip——root of tongue.
Imagination——Bartholomew——between the eyes.
Understanding——Thomas——front brain.
Will——Matthew——center front brain.
Order——James, son of Alphaeus——navel.
Zeal——Simon the Cananaean——back head, medulla.
Renunciation or Elimination——Thaddaeus——abdominal region.
Life Conserver——Judas——generative function.

The physiological designations of these faculties are not arbitrary—the names can be expanded or changed to suit a broader understanding of their full nature. For example, Philip, at the root of the tongue, governs taste; he also controls the action of the larynx, as well as all vibrations of power throughout the organism. So the term "power" expresses but a small part of his official capacity.

The first apostle that Jesus called was Peter. Peter represents faith in things spiritual, faith in God. We begin our religious experience, our unity with Divine Mind, by having faith in that mind as omnipresent, all-wise, all-loving, all-powerful Spirit.

Faith in the spiritual man quickens spiritual understanding. Peter believed that Jesus was the Messiah; his faith opened his spiritual discernment, and he saw the living Christ back of the personal mask worn by Jesus. When asked, "Who do men say that the Son of man is?" the apostles, looking upon personality as the real, said: "Some *say* John the Baptist; some, Elijah; and others, Jeremiah, or one of the prophets." Then Jesus appealed to their own inner spiritual understanding and He said: "But who say ye that I am?" Only Simon Peter answered: "Thou art the Christ, the Son of the living God." And Jesus answered, "Thou art Peter, and upon this rock I will build my church, and the gates of Hades [the grave] shall not prevail against it. I will give unto thee the keys of the kingdom of heaven."

Spiritual discernment of the reality of man's origin and being is the only enduring foundation of character. It was to this faith in the understanding of the real being of man that Jesus gave power in earth and heaven. It was not to the personal Peter that Jesus gave the keys to His kingdom, but to all who through faith apply the binding (affirming) and loosing (denying) power of Spirit in the earth (substance consciousness). Right here and now the great work of character-building is to be done, and whoever neglects present opportunities, looking forward to a future heaven for better conditions, is pulling right away from the kingdom of heaven within himself.

People who live wholly in the intellect deny that man can know anything about God, because they do not have quickened faith. The way to bring forth the God presence, to make oneself conscious of God, is to say: *I have faith in God; I have faith in Spirit; I have faith in things invisible.* Such affirmations of faith, such praise to the invisible God, the unknown God, will make God visible to the mind and will strengthen the faith faculty. Thus faith (Peter) is called and instructed spiritually.

When a center loses its power it should be baptized by the word of Spirit. We are told in the Scriptures that Philip went down to Gaza ("the same is desert"), and there baptized a eunuch. Gaza means a "citadel of strength." It refers to the nerve center in the loins, where Andrew (strength) reigns. "Lo now, his strength is in his loins." Gaza is the physical throne of strength, as Jerusalem is the throne of love.

The back grows weak under the burden of material thought. If you are given to pains in your back, if you become exhausted easily, you may know at once that you need treatment for freedom from material burdens. Eliminate from your mind all thought of the burdens of the world, the burdens of your life, and all seeming labors. Take your burdens to Christ. "Come unto me, all ye that labor and are heavy laden, and I will give you rest."

We are pressed upon by ideas of materiality. Thoughts make things, and the material ideas that are pressing upon us are just as substantial in the realm of mind as material things are substantial in the realm of matter. Everything has origin in thought, and material thoughts will bring forth material things. So you should baptize and cleanse with your spiritual word every center, as Philip baptized the eunuch of Gaza. Baptism is cleansing. It always represents the erasing power of the mind.

When the baptizing power of the word is poured upon a center, it cleanses all material thought; impotence is vitalized with new life, and the whole subconsciousness is awakened and quickened. The word of the Lord is there sown in the body, and once the word of the Lord is sown in any of these centers—the cells of which are like blank phonograph records—they take the thought that is given them, and send it through the whole organism. The baptism of strength goes to the uttermost parts of the body, and every one of the twelve powers, under the divine law, feels the new strength.

James, the son of Zebedee, represents discrimination and good judgment in dealing with substantial things. James is the faculty in man that wisely chooses and determines. It may be in the matter of food; it may be in the matter of judgment about the relation of external forces; it may be in the choosing of a wife or a husband—in a thousand different ways this faculty is developed in man. The spiritual side of the James faculty is intuition, quick knowing.

James and John are brothers, and Jesus called them "sons of thunder." These brothers preside over the great body brain called the solar plexus, or sun center. James has his throne at the pit of the stomach; and John, just back of the heart. They are unified by bundles of nerves and are metaphysically closely related. Whatever affects the stomach will sympathetically affect the heart. People with weak stomachs nearly always think they have heart trouble.

Jesus called those two apostles "sons of thunder" because tremendous vibrations or emotions go forth from the solar plexus. When your sympathies are aroused, you will find that you begin to breathe deeply and strongly, and if you are very sympathetic you can feel the vibrations as they go out to the person or thing to which you are directing your thoughts. All fervor, all the high energy that comes from soul, passes through these centers.

Bartholomew represents the imagination. The imagination has its center of action directly between the eyes. This is the point of expression for a set of tissues that extend back into the brain and connect with an imaging or picture-making function near the root of the optic nerve. Through this faculty you can project an image of things that are without or ideas that are within. For instance, you can project the image of jealousy to any part of your body and, by the chemistry of thought combined with function, make your complexion yellow, or you can image and project beauty by thinking goodness and perfection for everybody. Bartholomew is connected directly with the soul, and has great power in the pictures of the mind. Jesus saw him under a fig tree, a long way off, before he was visible to the natural eye. Do not imagine anything but good, because under the law of thought combined with substance it will sooner or later come into expression, unless you head it off, eliminate it by denial.

Man has faculties of elimination, as well as of appropriation. If you know how to handle them you can expel error from your thought body. The denial apostle is Thaddaeus, presiding in the abdominal region, the great renunciator of the mind and the body. All the faculties are necessary to the perfect expression of the man. None is despised or unclean. Some have been misunderstood; through ignorance man has called them mean, until they act in that way and cause him pain and sorrow. The elimination, by Thaddaeus, of the waste of the system through the bowels is a very necessary function.

Thomas represents the understanding power of man. He is called the doubter because he wants to know about everything. Thomas is in the front brain, and his collaborator, Matthew, the will, occupies the same brain area. These two faculties are jointly in occupation of this part of the "promised land." Like the land of Ephraim and Manasseh, their inheritance is undivided.

James, the son of Alphaeus, represents divine order. His center is at the navel.

Simon, the Cananaean, represents zeal; his center is at the medulla, at the base of the brain. When you burn with zeal and are anxious to accomplish great things, you generate heat at the base of your brain. If this condition is not balanced by the cooperation of the supplying faculties, you will burn up the cells and impede the growth of the soul. "For the zeal of thy house hath eaten me up."

Judas, who betrayed Jesus, has his throne in the generative center. Judas governs the life consciousness in the body, and without his wise cooperation the organism loses its essential substance, and dies. Judas is selfish; greed is his "devil." Judas governs the most subtle of the "beasts of the field"—sensation; but Judas can be redeemed. The Judas function generates the life of the body. We need life, but life must be guided in divine ways. There must be a righteous expression of life. Judas, the betrayer of Jesus, must in the end be cleansed of the devil, selfishness; having been cleansed, he will allow the life force to flow to every part of the organism. Instead of being a thief (drawing to the sex center the vital forces necessary to the substance of the whole man) Judas will become a supplier; he will give his life to every faculty. In the prevailing race consciousness Judas drains the whole man, and the body dies as a result of his selfish thievery.

It is through Judas (the desire to appropriate and to experience the pleasure of sensation) that the soul (Eve) is led into sin. Through the sins of the sex life (casting away of the precious substance), the body is robbed of its essential fluids and eventually disintegrates. The result is called death, which is the great and last enemy to be overcome by man. Immortality in the body is possible to man only when he has overcome the weaknesses of sensation, and conserves his life substance. When we awaken to the realization that all indulgence for pleasure alone is followed by pain, then we shall know the meaning of eating of the tree of the knowledge of good and evil, or pleasure and pain.

If you would build up your faculties under the divine law, redeem Judas. First have faith in the power of Spirit, and then speak to Judas the word of purity. Speak to him the word of unselfishness; baptize him with the whole Spirit—Holy Spirit. If there is in you a selfish desire to exercise sensation, to experience the pleasures of sense in any of its avenues, give that desire to the Lord; in no other way can you come into eternal life.

These twelve powers are all expressed and developed under the guidance of Divine Mind. "Not by might, nor by power, but by my Spirit, saith Jehovah of hosts." You must keep the equipoise; you must, in all the bringing forth of the twelve powers of man, realize that they come from God: that they are directed by the Word of God, and that man (Jesus) is their head.

CHAPTER 2

The Development of Faith

FAITH has an abiding place in man's consciousness. This place of abiding is described in the Scriptures as the "house of Simon and Andrew." A house is a structure that some person has built for a home. A man's house is his castle. Perhaps generation after generation is born and reared in the same house. The house where a great genius was born is preserved with care, and it is visited year after year by those who are devotees of the one who expressed some great thought, art, or discovery. If the barn cave at Bethlehem, where Jesus was born, were found, it would become the most famous shrine in the world. The importance that we give to the places where great men and women were born is founded on the centralizing power of thought. All structures are thought concentrations. Constructive thinking ultimates in the construction of places of abode. Savages do not build houses or cities, because they do not think constructively.

In the time of David the Children of Israel were nomads. The consciousness of indwelling Spirit had not been born in their minds, and could not, in consequence, be formed in their bodies. That the time was ripe for a more constructive state of mind is set forth in these words of Jehovah, in 2 Samuel 7:5–6:

24

"Shalt thou build me a house for me to dwell in? for I have not dwelt in a house since the day that I brought up the children of Israel out of Egypt, even to this day, but have walked in a tent and in a tabernacle."

After receiving this message, David, the drawing power of love, began gathering material for Solomon's Temple. Jehovah told David that he could not build the Temple because he was a man of war. The temple of God is man's body ("Your body is a temple of the Holy Spirit"), but if man has not complied with the law of permanent body building, he is like the nomadic Children of Israel: he goes from body to body and from tabernacle to tabernacle.

> Except Jehovah build the house,
> They labor in vain that build it.

The tents and the tabernacles that the Children of Israel built for Jehovah represent the transitory bodies of flesh. The Lord has merely "walked" in these flimsy temples; they have not afforded an abiding place for Spirit, because of their unsubstantial character. The underlying weakness of the tent body was its lack of faith in the inhabiting soul. A new consciousness of the indwelling spiritual substance and life was necessary, and a man was chosen to bring it forth. This man, named Abraham, represents obedience and faith. His original name was Abram, which means "exalted father." The name is identified with the highest cosmic principle, the all-pervading, self-existent spiritual substance, which is the primary source of the universe.

Abraham was tested again and again, to the end

that he might be strong in faith. His great test of faith was his willingness to sacrifice his beloved son Isaac on the mountain of the Lord. "And Abraham called the name of that place Jehovah-jireh: as it is said to this day, In the mount of Jehovah it shall be provided."

This incident is intended to show the necessity of a man's giving up that which he considers his dearest possession before he can realize the divine providence. The incident takes place on the mount of the Lord; that is, in a high spiritual understanding.

The law of giving and receiving pertains to the realm of ideas; one must give up personal attachments before one can receive the universal. If a parent idealizes a child, loves it so dearly that its pleasure is first in the parent's consciousness, the spiritual development of the parent is impeded. Then, before the love of God (which is the supreme thing) can fill the heart, there must be a sacrifice of human love. If like Abraham one is faithful and obedient and willing to give to the Lord his most precious possession, there is always a receiving or providing equivalent.

When Abraham was willing to sacrifice his beloved Isaac, the Lord stayed his hand; his attention was directed to a ram in a thicket nearby, and he was directed to sacrifice the animal upon the altar, in place of the child. Here is illustrated an often misunderstood law of sacrifice or renunciation. We do not have to give up our cherished things, if they are real, but the error that prevents their full expression must be destroyed. The ram (which represents the resistance and opposition of personality to the complete expression of Truth) must be sacrificed.

"Give, and it shall be given unto you" is the statement of a law that operates in every thought and act of man. This law is the foundation of all barter and financial exchange. Men scheme to get something for nothing; but the law, in one of its many forms, overtakes them in the end. Even metaphysicians, who above all people should understand the law, often act as if they expected God to provide abundantly for them before they have earned abundance. It is an error to think that God gives anybody anything that has not been earned. The Holy Spirit comes upon those who pray in the "upper room." The "upper room" corresponds to the "mount of Jehovah." It is the high place in consciousness where man realizes the presence of Divine Mind. The greatest work that one can do is to strive to know God and to keep His law. God pays liberally for this service and the reward is sure. Faith is built up in consciousness under this law.

"Faith is assurance of *things* hoped for." When there has been an aspiration and a reaching out for the spiritual life, the faith faculty becomes active in consciousness. The prayer of supplication is impotent—the prayer of affirmation is immediately effective.

Intellectual faith admits doubt, and hope of fulfillment in the future; spiritual faith includes unfail-

ing assurance and immediate response. These two
attitudes of faith are often observed acting and re-
acting upon each other. Peter started to walk on
the water in spiritual faith, but when he saw the effects of the wind he was afraid and began to sink.
Then the I AM (Jesus) gave its hand of spiritual
power, the wind ceased, and there was no longer
any doubt of faith's ability to rise above the negative
consciousness.

The first and greatest disciple of Jesus was Peter,
who has been universally accepted by the followers
of Jesus the Christ as a type representing faith. Before he met Jesus, Peter was called Simon. *Simon*
means "hearing," which represents receptivity. We
understand from this that listening to Truth in a receptive state of mind opens the way for receiving the
next degree in the divine order, which is faith. Jesus
gave Peter his new name and also its meaning: "Thou
art Peter, and upon this rock I will build my church."

Faith in the reality of the invisible builds a real,
abiding substance in mind and in body. All kinds of
ideas grow quickly when planted in this rich substance of the mind. Jesus also called this substance
of faith the "earth," and He said to Peter, "Whatsoever thou shalt bind [affirm] on earth shall be
bound in heaven; and whatsoever thou shalt loose
[deny] on earth shall be loosed in heaven." In all
His teaching Jesus emphasized that the ruling forces
of both heaven and earth are in man. "The kingdom
of God is within you." "All authority hath been
given unto me in heaven and on earth." "Is it not

written in your law, I said, Ye are gods?" When we understand the omnipresence of Spirit (God) we quickly see how simple and true this beautiful doctrine of Jesus is.

There is but one real faith; the avenue of expression determines the character and power of faith. Trust is a cheaper brand of faith, but trust is better than mistrust. As a rule, people who merely trust in the Lord do not understand all the law. If they had understanding they would affirm the presence and power of God until the very substance of Spirit would appear in consciousness—and this is faith established on a rock.

Faith words should be expressed both silently and audibly. The power of the spoken word is but slightly understood, because the law of the Word is not rightly observed. The Word is the creative idea in Divine Mind, which may be expressed by man when he has fulfilled the law of expression. All words are formative but not all words are creative. The creative word lays hold of Spirit substance and power. Physical science hints at this inner substance and energy in its description of the almost inconceivable power inherent in the universal ether. We are told that the manifest forces, such as heat, light, and electricity, are but faint manifestations of an omnipresent element which is thousands of times greater than these weak expressions.

Radio is opening up a new field of activity in the use of the spoken word. A newspaper article on the wireless telephone says:

Do you happen to know that a single word spoken in
Lower Broadway, New York, among the skyscrapers, could
break every pane of glass in adjacent buildings and create a disturbance that would be felt for a mile in every direction?

The human voice, transformed into electrical energy for
wireless transmission, develops 270 horse power. The power of
ten men is equal to one horse power. The human voice electrified for wireless purposes is equivalent to the power of
2,700 men. In the various processes that step up a voice for
radio transmission across the Atlantic ocean, it becomes
135,000 times more powerful than when uttered by the person sending the message.

Thus, starting with an initial energy of 1/1,000 of an
electric watt, the voice is boosted by a powerful station until
it is intensified 100 million times.

If the spoken word can be mechanically intensified a hundred million times, how much greater will
be its power when energized by Spirit! When Jesus
said with a loud voice to Lazarus, "Come forth,"
He must have made contact with the creative word
referred to in the first chapter of John, because the
results showed its life-giving character. When He
healed the centurion's servant by His word sent
forth on invisible currents, He said that the work
was done through faith. So faith must boost the
spoken word even more than a hundred million
times as evidenced by its marvelous results. That
the word of faith has an inner force, and that this
force rushes forth and produces remarkable trans-
formations in the phenomenal world, is the testimony of thousands who have witnessed its results.

Jesus said: "If ye have faith as a grain of mustard seed, ye shall say unto this mountain, Remove hence to yonder place; and it shall remove; and nothing shall be impossible unto you." He knew about the great spiritual machinery that the word of faith sets into action. He illustrated how man spiritually developed could by faith control the elements, quell storms, walk on water, retard or increase the growth of life and substance in grains, trees, animals, and men.

The ponderous dynamos that generate electricity to light a city are set going by a touch of a button. There is a button in the mind of man that connects him, through faith, with almighty energy. When the word of faith is spoken to large tumors and they melt away, is not the transformation equal to the removal of mountains? When a paralyzed limb, or a lifeless organ, is quickened and restored to natural functioning, is not that quickening a raising of the dead?

It is not necessary that the one who touches the button of faith shall understand all the intricate machinery with which he makes contact; he knows, like one who turns the electric switch, that the light or power will spring forth. The faith center, the pineal gland, opens the mind of man to spiritual faith. Merely affirming the activity of this superpower will quicken it in consciousness. Jesus said, "I speak not from myself: but the Father [faith] abiding in me doeth his works."

The transformers of electricity are paralleled by the transforming power of mind. That if a man

sanely believes he can do a thing he will eventually
find a way to do it is an accepted axiom of psychology. The mind generates an energy that contacts
the universal energy and causes circumstances and
events to fall into line for the attainment of the latent ideal. John came crying in the wilderness of
mortal thought, "Repent ye"; that is, change your
mind. Paul discerned a like necessity, hence his call:
"Be ye transformed by the renewing of your mind."

When people see the possibilities that follow a
right change of mind, they will crowd the halls of
metaphysical teachers as they now crowd moving
picture shows. When it is clearly understood that
doubt, fear, poverty, disease, and death—every
thought, good or bad, that men have expressed—
have existence through mind, we shall see a shifting
of consciousness and a radical change in thought and
word by everybody of sane mind. Then we shall ask
for the true source and find it, as did Paul, who
said: "Have this mind in you, which was also in
Christ Jesus." It was not Jesus but the mind in
Jesus that did the great works. He was the center
of faith that transformed the mighty creative forces
of Being (which are active in the universe through
the mind and brain of man) into a form of force
usable in His environment. Tap this inner reservoir
of faith and you can do what Jesus did. That
was His promise; its fulfillment is the test of a true
follower.

"By faith Enoch was translated that he should
not see death . . . . By faith Noah . . . prepared an

ark to the saving of his house . . . . By faith Abraham, being tried, offered up Isaac . . . . By faith Moses, when he was born, was hid three months by his parents . . . . By faith the walls of Jericho fell down . . . . And what shall I more say? for the time will fail me if I tell of Gideon, Barak, Samson, Jephthah; of David and Samuel and the prophets: who through faith subdued kingdoms, wrought righteousness, obtained promises, stopped the mouths of lions, quenched the power of fire, escaped the edge of the sword, from weakness were made strong, waxed mighty in war, turned to flight armies of aliens. Women received their dead by a resurrection."

CHAPTER 3

Strength—Stability—Steadfastness

WHEN the strong *man* fully armed guardeth his own court, his goods are in peace: but when a stronger than he shall come upon him, and overcome him, he taketh from him his whole armor wherein he trusted, and divideth his spoils.

Jesus gave the foregoing illustration of a strong man's being overcome by a stronger. The incident is mentioned in three of the Gospels, those of Matthew, Mark, and Luke. It is usually interpreted as illustrating in a general way the overcoming of evil, but the peculiar identification of the strong man in his court (or house), and the necessity of overcoming him, hint at a deeper significance. One who has studied man as an aggregation of personalities readily identifies the "strong man" as one of the twelve foundation powers that make up the manifest man. Among the apostles of Jesus, the strong man is designated as Andrew, brother of Peter. The Greek meaning of *Andrew* is "strong man."

The development of the natural world from coarser to finer types in vegetable life and in animal life is paralleled in many respects in the unfoldment of man. The source of everything is in the realm of ideas; a knowledge of this fact, coupled with faith

34

in the working power of the unseen, makes man greater than all other expressions of Divine Mind. However, knowledge of the law of mind evolution does not relieve man of the necessity of refining and transmuting the various types of man that he has brought forth, and of which he is the epitome.

The Jehovah man is constantly making the Adam man and breathing into his nostrils the breath of life. The Adam man exists in the subconsciousness as a multitude of men: The wise man and the foolish man, the kind man and the cruel man, the loving man and the hateful man, the stingy man and the generous man, the hungry man and the full man, the happy man and the troubled man, the weak man and the strong man, the good man and the bad man, the live man and the dead man, the poor man and the rich man, the timid man and the courageous man, the sick man and the healthy man, the old man and the young man, the erratic man and the sane man—these, and a thousand other types of man as active personalities, occupy the consciousness of every human being. Every male has within him the female, and every female has within her the male. This fact is admitted by physiology, substantiating the Genesis record of the ideal creation of man as "male and female," and his expression in Adam and Eve as the male and female in one man. The fact was corroborated by the Great Teacher when He said, "Have ye not read, that he who made *them* from the beginning made them male and female?"

The "strong *man* fully armed," referred to by

Jesus, is the strength and stability in man. In the natural man he is manifest as physical strength, but in the regeneration he is overcome and his possessions are divided or given to the other faculties as a nucleus around which the higher forces gather. The "stronger than he" who takes away the "whole armor" in which the strong man trusted is spiritual strength. The overcoming of Goliath by David illustrates the mastery of the spiritual over the material. Goliath trusted in his armor, which represents the protective power of matter and material conditions. David, spiritual strength, had no armor or material protection. David's power was gained by trust in divine intelligence, through which he saw the weak place in Goliath's armor. Direct to this weak place, with the sling of his concentrated will, he sent a thought that shattered the forehead of the giant. This incident shows how easy it is to overcome the seemingly strong personal and material conditions when the mind of Spirit is brought into action.

David was sure of himself, because he had slain the lion that had killed his sheep. The lion is the beast in man; when overcome or, rather, transmuted to finer energy, this lion becomes a mighty soul strength.

The life of Samson, as set forth in Judges, shows the different movements of strength in human consciousness, and its betrayal and end. Samson did all kinds of athletic stunts, but was finally robbed of his strength by Delilah, a Philistine woman, who had his head shaved while he slept on her knees. Hair represents vitality. When the vital principle is taken away the strength goes with it. The body is weakened by this devitalization and finally perishes. Eve took away the strength of Adam in like manner, and every man who gives up the vital essence of his body for the pleasure of sensation blindly pulls down the pillar of his temple, as did Samson.

Supreme strength as demonstrated by Jesus can be attained by one who trusts in Spirit and conserves his vital substance. The strength of Spirit is necessary to the perpetuation of soul and body and to the overcoming of death. "For there are eunuchs, that were so born from their mother's womb: and there are eunuchs, that were made eunuchs by men: and there are eunuchs, that made themselves eunuchs for the kingdom of heaven's sake."

The body has many "brain" and nerve centers through which the mind acts. Consciously we use only the brain in the head. We should think through every cell in the organism, and consciously direct every function in building up the body. When one has attained the mastery of these various bodily functions through thinking in the brain center that stores the vital energy of each particular faculty, then all deterioration ceases and the body is perpetually renewed.

The strength here discussed is not physical strength alone, but mental and spiritual strength. All strength originates in Spirit; and the thought and the word spiritually expressed bring the manifestation. "The name of Jehovah is a strong tower."

We grow to be like that which we idealize. Affirming or naming a mighty spiritual principle identifies the mind with that principle; then all that the principle stands for in the realm of ideas is poured out upon the one who affirms.

"Be strong in the Lord, and in the strength of his might" is a great strengthening affirmation for ourselves and for others. Be steadfast, strong, and steady in thought, and you will establish strength in mind and in body. Never let the thought of weakness enter your consciousness, but always ignore the suggestion and affirm yourself to be a tower of strength, within and without.

The development of man is under law. Creative Mind is not only law, but it is governed by the action of the law that it sets up. We have thought that man was brought forth under the fiat or edict of a great creative Mind that could make or unmake at will, or change its mind and declare a new law at any time; but a clear understanding of ourselves and of the unchangeableness of Divine Mind makes us realize that everything has its foundation in a rule of action, a law, that must be observed by both creator and created.

Man's development is not primarily under the physical law, because the physical law is secondary. There is a law of Spirit, and the earthly is but the showing forth of some of the results of that law. We begin our existence as ideas in Divine Mind; those ideas are expressed and developed and brought to fruitage, and the expression is the important part of the soul's growth.

Evolution is the result of the development of ideas in mind. What we are is the result of the evolution of our consciousness, and that consciousness is the result of seed ideas sown in our mind. When Froebel, the great teacher of children, began his primary school, he thought a long time before he gave it a name. One day the name came to him: "a children's garden"; so he called his school a "kindergarten." Froebel may not have seen the connection, but in naming his system of educating the children of men, he was true to the plan given in Genesis 2:8. Humanity is the garden of God, of which the soil is the omnipresent thought substance.

Jesus says that the seed is the word; He gives illustrations of the various places in which the seed is sown, and the results of the sowing. The seed, or Word of God, is sown in the minds of men; these seed ideas go through many changes, and they bring forth a harvest according to the capacity of the receiving soil. If you will to do the will of God, the exercise of your will in God-Mind strengthens your will power. If you have faith in things invisible, the faith seed is growing in your mind and your faith will be increased. Every word or idea in Divine Mind is sown by man in his mind, and is then brought forth—according to man's receptivity. "Whatsoever a man soweth, that shall he also reap." So all the faculties that exist in Divine Mind (the twelve pillars of the temple of God) are in this way expressed through the mind and the body of man.

Some have claimed that the Bible is a work on physiology. So it is, but it is far more; it treats of Spirit, soul, and body as a unit. That is the reason why those who have studied the Bible from a merely physiological standpoint have not understood it. They have looked for descriptions of flesh and bones. In truth those things have no active existence without accompanying life and intelligence; and the Bible sets forth this fact in many symbols.

Jesus, the Great Teacher, who knew what was in man, began His evolution with Spirit. He is the "only begotten Son of God"; He is the type that you should strive to follow, not only in spiritual culture and in soul culture, but in physical culture. If you would bring forth the very best that is in you, study the methods of Jesus. Study them in all their details, get at the spirit of everything that is written about this wonderful man, and you will find the key to the true development of your soul and your body. If you will carry out His system, there will be revealed to you a new man, a man of whom you never dreamed, existing in the hidden realms of your own subconsciousness.

CHAPTER 4

Wisdom—Judgment

WHICH is the greater, wisdom or love? After long study of the analysis of love given by Paul in the thirteenth chapter of 1 Corinthians, Henry Drummond pronounced love to be "the greatest thing in the world." His conclusion is based on Paul's setting forth of the virtues of love. Had wisdom been as well championed as love was, the author of *The Greatest Thing in the World* might not have been so sure of his ground. It goes without argument that love wins when everything else fails, but notwithstanding her mightiness, she makes many blunders. Love will make any and every sacrifice for the thing that she loves; on the other hand, she is enticed into trap after trap in her blind search for pleasure. It was this kind of love that caused Eve to fall under the spell of sensation, the serpent. She saw that the fruit of the tree was "pleasant to the eyes." She followed the pleasure of life instead of the wisdom that would have shown her how to use life. Ever since, we have had pleasure and pain, or good and evil, as the result of Eve's blind love.

What kind of people would we be if Eve and Adam had been obedient to the Lord of wisdom, instead of obeying the sense of love? This is one

of the biggest questions that anyone can ask. It has
been debated for many, many centuries. It has a
double answer. Those who get the first answer will
claim that it is correct, and those who get the second answer will assure you that there can be no
other conclusion. The question hinges on one point,
and that is: Must one experience evil in order to appreciate good? If it were possible for man to know
all the wisdom and joy of the Infinite, he would
have no necessity for experience with the opposite.
But do we have to have pain before we can enjoy
pleasure? Does the child that burns its hand on a hot
stove have a larger consciousness of health when the
hand is healed? Has it learned more about stoves?
Unnumbered illustrations of this kind might be
given to show that by experimentation we learn the
relations existing between things in the phenomenal world. But if we apply this rule to sciences that
are governed by absolute rules, it becomes evident
that there is no necessity for knowing the negative.
To become proficient in mathematics, it is not necessary that one makes errors. The more closely one
follows the rules in exact sciences, the more easily
and successfully one makes the demonstrations. This
goes to prove that the nearer one comes to the absolute or cause side of existence, the greater is one's
understanding that wisdom and order rule, and
that he who joins wisdom and order rules with them.

God knows that there is a great negative, which
is a reflection of His positive, but He is not *conscious*
of its existence. We know that there is an under-

world of evil, in which all the rules of civilized life are broken, but we are not *conscious* of that world because we do not enter into it. It is one thing to view error as a thing apart from us, and quite another to enter into consciousness of it. In the allegory of Adam and Eve, the man and the woman were told by wisdom not to "eat" (not to enter into consciousness of the fruit of the tree of knowledge of good and evil). But the pleasure of sensation (serpent) tempted them, and they ate.

Sensation, feeling, affection, and love are closely allied. Sensation is personified in the Edenic allegory as the serpent, the most subtle of the beasts of the field (animal forces alive in substance). The subtlety of sensation in its various guises is in its pleasure, the thrill that comes when mind and matter join in the ecstasy of life. When the desire for the pleasures of sensation is indulged and the guiding wisdom ignored, a realm of consciousness is established that regards the material universe as the only reality. The Lord, the knowing side of man, talks to him in the "cool of the day." In the heat of passion and the joy of pleasure, man does not listen to the "still, small voice," but in the "cool of the day," that is, when he cools off, he reflects, and he hears the voice of wisdom and judgment saying: "Where art thou, Adam ?"

The "great day of judgment"—which has been located at some fateful time in the future when we all shall be called before the judge of the world and have punishment meted out to us for our sins

—is every day. The translators of the Authorized
Version and of the American Standard Version of
the New Testament are responsible for the "great
judgment day" bugaboo. In every instance where
judgment was mentioned by Jesus, He said "in a day
of judgment," but the translators changed *a* to *the,*
making the time of judgment appear a definite
point in the future, instead of the repeated con-
summations of causes that occur in the lives of individuals and nations. We know that we are constantly being brought to judgment for transgressing
the laws—moral and physical. Yet back of these is
the spiritual law, which the whole race has broken
and for which we suffer. It was to mend the results
of this lawbreaking that Jesus was incarnated.

When we awaken to the reality of our being, the
light begins to break upon us from within and we
know the truth; this is the quickening of our James
or judgment faculty. When this quickening occurs,
we find ourselves discriminating between the good
and the evil. We no longer accept the race standards
or the teachings of the worldly wise, but we "judge
righteous judgment"; we know with an inner intuition, and we judge men and events from a new viewpoint. "Knowledge comes but wisdom lingers," sings
the poet. This pertains to intellectual development
only. When man kindles the inner light, he speaks
the word of authority to his subjective faculties. Jesus
represents the Son-of-God consciousness in man, to
whom was given dominion over all the earth. The
Son-of-God man is wholly spiritual, and he uses

spiritual thoughts, words, and laws in all that he does.

When Jesus called the Twelve, He spoke silently to the faculties that preside over and direct the functions of mind and body. When He called Peter, James, and John, there was in His consciousness a quickening of faith, judgment, and love. These three apostles are mentioned more often than His other apostles because they are most essential in the expression of a well-balanced man. Andrew (strength) was also among the first few called; he represents the stability that lies at the foundation of every true character.

"James the Just" was the title bestowed by historians upon the first bishop of Jerusalem. There were many Jameses among the early followers of Jesus, and there is some doubt as to whether James the Just and James the apostle are identical.

An analysis of man in his threefold nature reveals that on every plane there is a certain reflective and discerning power of the mind and its thoughts. In the body, conclusions are reached through experience; in intellect, reason is the assumed arbiter of every question; in Spirit, intuition and inspiration bring the quick and sure answer to all the problems of life. Jesus was the greatest of the teachers of men, because He knew all knowledge, from the highest to the lowest. He did not blight the senses by calling them "error" (because they are limited in their range of vision), but He lifted them up. He took Peter, James, and John up into the mountain, and was transfigured before them. When we realize the spiritual possibilities with which we are indued by omnipotent Mind, we are lifted up, and all the faculties that we have "called" are lifted up with us. "I, if I be raised on high from the earth, will draw all to myself" (Diaglott).

Wisdom, justice, judgment, are grouped under one head in spiritual consciousness. Webster says in effect that the ground of reason in judgment, which makes conclusions *knowledge,* is found in the connecting link that binds the conceptions together. In religion there is the postulate of a judgment through direct perception of the divine law.

Solomon (Sol-o-mon), the sun man, or solar plexus man, when asked by the Lord what He should give him, chose wisdom above riches and honor; then all the other things were added. Solomon was also a great judge. He had a rare intuition, and he used it freely in arriving at his judgments. He did not rest his investigations on mere facts, but sought out the inner motives. In the case of the two women who claimed the same infant, he commanded an attendant to bring a sword and cut the child in twain and give a half to each woman. Of course the real mother begged him not to do this, and he knew at once that she was the mother.

The appeal of the affectional nature in man for judgment in its highest is in harmony with divine law. We have thought that we were not safe in trusting our feelings to guide us in important issues. But spiritual discernment shows that the "quick-knowing" power of man has its seat of action in the breast. The breastplates worn by Jewish high priests had twelve stones, representing the twelve great powers of the mind. Ready insight into the divine law was the glory of the high priest. Jesus is called the high priest of God, and every man's name is the name *Jesus,* written large or small, according to his perception of his Son-of-God nature.

Intuition, judgment, wisdom, justice, discernment, pure knowing, and profound understanding are natural to man. All these qualities, and many more, belong to every one of us by and through his divine sonship. "I said, Ye are gods, and all of you sons of the Most High!" the Christ proclaims in us all. Paul saw Christ waiting at the door of every soul, when he wrote: "Awake, thou that sleepest, and arise from the dead, and Christ shall shine upon thee."

A quickening of our divine judgment arouses in us the judge of all the world. "The wisdom that is from above is first pure, then peaceable." When we call this righteous judge into action, we may find our standards of right and wrong undergoing rapid changes, but if we hold steadily to the Lord as our supreme guide, we shall be led into all righteousness.

Many persons doubt that there is an infinite law of justice working in all things; let them now take heart and know that this law has not worked in their affairs previously because they have not "called" it into activity in the creative center of the soul. When we call our inner forces into action, the universal law begins its great work in us, and all the laws, both great and small, fall into line and work for us. We do not make the law; the law *is,* and it was established for our benefit before the world was formed. Jesus did not make the law of health when He healed the multitudes; He simply called it into expression by getting it recognized by those who had disregarded its existence. Back of the judge is the law out of which he reads. This fact is recognized even by those who are intrusted with the carrying out of man-made laws. Blackstone says that the judgment, though pronounced and awarded by the judges, is not their determination or sentence, but the determination and sentence of the law. So we who are carrying forward the fulfillment of the law as inaugurated by Jesus should be wise in recognizing that the law in all its fullness already exists right here, waiting for us to identify ourselves with it and thus allow it to fulfill its righteousness in us and in all the world.

"I am the vine, ye are the branches." In this symbol Jesus illustrated a law universal to organisms. The vine-building law holds good in man's body. The center of identity is in the head, and its activities are distributed through the nerves and the nerve fluids to the various parts of the body. The Twelve Apostles of Jesus Christ represent the twelve primal subcenters in man's organism. A study of man's mind and body reveals this law.

Even physiologists, who regard the body as a mere physical organism, find certain aggregations of cells which they have concluded are for no other purpose than for the distribution of intelligence. To one who studies man as mind, these aggregations of cells are regarded as the avenues through which certain fundamental ideas are manifested. We name these ideas "the twelve powers of man," identified in man's consciousness as the Twelve Apostles of Jesus, having twelve houses, villages, cities, or centers in the body through which they act.

Wisdom includes judgment, discrimination, intuition, and all the departments of mind that come under the head of knowing. The house or throne of this wise judge is at the nerve center called the solar plexus. The natural man refers to it as the pit of the stomach. The presiding intelligence at this center knows what is going on, especially in the domain of consciousness pertaining to the body and its needs. Chemistry is its specialty; it also knows all that pertains to the sensations of soul and body. In its highest phase it makes union with the white light of Spirit functioning in the top brain. At the solar plexus also takes place the union between love and wisdom. The apostle who has charge of this center is called James. Volumes might be written describing the activities by which this power builds and preserves man's body. Every bit of food that we take into our stomachs must be intelligently and chemically treated at this center before it can be distributed to the many members waiting for this center's wise judgment to supply them with material to build bone, muscle, nerve, eye, ear, hair, nails—in fact every part of the organism. When we study the body and its manifold functions we see how much depends on the intelligence and ability of James, who functions through the solar plexus.

When man begins to follow Jesus in the regeneration, he finds that he must co-operate with the work of his disciples or faculties. Heretofore they have been under the natural law; they have been fishers in the natural world. Through his recognition of his relation as the Son of God, man co-operates in the original creative law. He calls his faculties out of their materiality into their spirituality. This process is symbolized by Jesus' calling His apostles.

To call a disciple is mentally to recognize that power; it is to identify oneself with the intelligence working at a center—for example, judgment, at the solar plexus. To make this identification, one must realize one's unity with God through Christ, Christ being the Son-of-God idea always existing in man's higher consciousness. This recognition of one's sonship and unity with God is fundamental in all true growth. Christ is the door into the kingdom of God. Jesus once spoke of the kingdom as a sheepfold. If man tries to get into this kingdom except through the door of the Christ, he is a thief and a robber. We can call our twelve powers into spiritual activity only through Christ. If we try to effect this end by any other means, we shall have an abnormal, chaotic, and unlawful soul unfoldment.

Having identified oneself with God through Christ, one should center one's attention at the pit of the stomach and affirm:

The wisdom of the Christ Mind here active is through my recognition of Christ identified and unified with God. Wisdom, judgment, discrimination, purity, and power are here now expressing themselves in the beauty of holiness. The justice, righteousness, and peace of the Christ Mind now harmonize, wisely direct, and surely establish the kingdom of God in His temple, my body. There are no more warring, contentious thoughts in me, for the peace of God is here established, and the lion and the lamb (courage and innocence) sit on the throne of dominion with wisdom and love.

CHAPTER 5

Regenerating Love

W E CANNOT get a right understanding of the relation that the manifest bears to the unmanifest, until we set clearly before ourselves the character of original Being. So long as we think of God in terms of personality, just so long shall we fail to understand the relation existing between man and God.

Then let us dismiss the thought that God is a man, or even a man exalted far above human characteristics. So long as the concept of a man-God exists in consciousness, there will be a lack of room for the true concept, which is that God is First Cause, the Principle from which flow all manifestations. To understand the complex conditions under which the human family exists, we must analyze Being and its creative processes.

Inherent in the Mind of Being are twelve fundamental ideas, which in action appear as primal creative forces. It is possible for man to ally himself with and to use these original forces, and thereby cooperate with the creative law, but in order to do this he must detach himself from the forces and enter into the consciousness of the idea lying back of them.

In Scripture the primal ideas in the Mind of Being are called the "sons of God." That the masculine "son" is intended to include both masculine and feminine is borne out by the context, and, in fact, the whole history of the race. Being itself must be masculine and feminine, in order to make man in its image and likeness, "male and female."

Analyzing these divine ideas, or sons of God, we find that they manifest characteristics that we readily identify as masculine or feminine. For example, life is a son of God, while love is a daughter of God. Intelligence is a son of God, and imagination is a daughter of God. The evidence that sex exists in the vegetable and animal worlds is so clear that it is never questioned, but we have not so clearly discerned that *ideas* are also male and female. The union of the masculine and feminine forces in man is most potent in the affectional nature, and that these forces should endure and never be separated by external causes was laid down as a law by Jesus. He said, as recorded in Mark 10:6-9:

"From the beginning of the creation, Male and female made he them. For this cause shall a man leave his father and mother, and shall cleave to his wife; and the two shall become one flesh: so that they are no more two, but one flesh. What therefore God hath joined together, let not man put asunder."

We should clearly understand that each of the various ideas, or sons and daughters of God, has identity and in creation is striving with divine might to bring forth its inherent attributes. It is to these ideas, or sons and daughters, that Being, or Elohim, says: "Let us make man in our image, after our likeness" (Gen. 1:26).

Spiritual man is the sum total of the attributes or perfect ideas of Being, identified and individualized. This man is the "only begotten" of Elohim. Jehovah, or I AM THAT I AM, is the name of this divine man. He was manifest as the higher self of Jesus, and in the Scriptures is called the Christ. Jesus named Him the "Father in me"; in the book of Matthew, He called Him "Father" more than forty times. Christ is our Father; through Him, Elohim or original Being brings forth all human beings. It was Jehovah, or I AM, that formed Adam out of the dust of the ground and breathed into his nostrils the breath of life. Breathing is the symbol of inspiration. Jesus breathed upon His disciples, and said to them: "Receive ye the Holy Spirit."

Three primal forces of Being are manifest in the simplest protoplastic cell. Science says that every atom has substance, life, and intelligence. This corresponds with the symbolical creative process of Jehovah, as described in Genesis 2:7. The "dust of the ground" is substance; "breathed" refers to the impartation of intelligence; and the "living soul" is the quickening life. These three constitute the trinity of the natural world, in which the body of man is cast. When one understands the creative processes to be the working of the various principles of Being in the development of man, many inexplicable situations are cleared up. God cannot bring forth without law and order. To produce a man, there must be a combination of forces that at some stages of soul evolution may seem to work against one another; but when one understands that the great creative Mind brings forth under law, reconciliation and consistency are found where inharmony and contradiction seemed dominant.

Of all the daughters of God, love is undoubtedly the most beautiful, enticing, and fascinating. She is by nature exceedingly timid and modest, but when roused she is bold and fearless in the extreme. Mother love is as strong as life and will make every sacrifice to protect offspring. This wholehearted, self-sacrificing aspect of love indicates a spirit deeper and stronger than the animal or the human, and we are forced to admit that it is divine. For this reason mother love is exalted to first place in our analysis of the great passion. But mothers should take heed lest they incorporate human selfishness into the divine love that is expressed in and through them.

The most popular expression of love in the world is the love between men and women. Here also love is misunderstood, and for that reason she has been forced to act in ways that are unnatural to her. She has also been compelled to do things that are abhorrent to her, yet under the compelling power of man's will she could not do otherwise. Right here is a crying need for a purer judgment of love and her right adjustment in the most sacred relation existing between men and women. Love is from God, and it is given to man in its virgin purity. It is the pure essence of Being that binds together the whole human family. Without love we should lose contact

with our mother earth, and losing that, we should
fly off into space and be lost in the star dust of unborn worlds. "Gravity" is mortal man's name for
love. By the invisible arms of love we are held tight
to earth's prolific bosom, and there we find the
sweetest home in all the universe. All love of home
is founded on man's innate love for this planet.
When John Howard Payne wrote "Home, Sweet
Home," he was inspired by mother love to sing of
the only abiding place of this race—our dear mother
earth.

The original Eden of the human family was
planted by God on earth, and it is still here. Its
prototype is within the human soul, but we have not
entered it, because we have not understood the relation that love bears to the original substance of
Being, out of which all things are formed.

It is no great task to tell of the higher aspects of
love, but who will champion love submerged in
human consciousness and smothered with selfishness? You say: "This is not love, but passion and
lust." But we should remember that we have laid
down, as a foundation principle, that God is love,
and, as there is but one God, there can be but one
love. This being true, we must find a place in the
creative law for every manifestation, regardless of its
apparent contradictions of the righteousness of First
Cause.

Love is submerged or cast down to sense consciousness between men and women in the marriage relation, and great misery floods the world in

consequence. This marriage should be a perpetual feast of love, and so it would be if the laws of love were observed. Courtship is usually the most joyous experience that comes to men and women, because love is kept free from lust.

If the laws of conjugality were better understood, the bliss of courtship would continue throughout all the years of married life and divorces would be unknown. It is a fact well known to psychologists that the majority of estrangements between husbands and wives result from the breaking of sex law. This sin that ends in feebleness and final disintegration of the physical organism is symbolically pictured in the so-called fall of man, in the early chapters of Genesis. Adam and Eve represent the innocent and uneducated powers of the masculine and feminine in every individual. The serpent symbolizes sensation, which combines with life and substance in all living organisms. The desire for pleasure, and for a seemingly short and easy way to get wisdom, tempts the feminine, and she eats, or appropriates. The masculine also eats. In the "cool of the day" (after the heat of passion has cooled off) they both find that they are naked. They have had pleasure with pleasure as the only object, which is contrary to the law of Being. All things should be done with a purpose, with pleasure as a concomitant only. Pleasure lends zest to all action, but it should never be exalted to the high place in consciousness.

Sex indulgence for mere pleasure is an eating or

appropriating of the pure substance that pervades the whole nervous system, which is appropriately compared to a tree. This excess of pleasure is sooner or later followed by equal reaction, which is destructive, and the body cries out in pain. The pleasure we call "good," and the pain we call "evil." Here, in a nutshell, is an explanation of eating of the tree of the "knowledge of good and evil."

When the substance in the organism is conserved and retained, the nerves are charged with a spiritual energy, which runs like lightning through an organism filled with the virgin substance of the soul. When, in the ignorance of sensation, men and women deplete their substance, the rose of the cheek and the sparkle of the eye fade away. Then the kiss and the touch that were once so satisfying become cold and lifeless.

In the conservation of this pure substance of life is hidden the secret of body rejuvenation, physical resurrection, and the final perpetuation of the whole organism in its transmuted purity. (John saw Jesus in this state of purity, as described in Revelation 1:12-16.) No man can in his own might attain this exalted estate, but through the love of God, demonstrated by Jesus, it is attainable by everyone. "For God so loved the world, that he gave his only begotten Son, that whosoever believeth on him should not perish, but have eternal life."

Regeneration is not possible without love. As through the union of the male and female elements the new body of the infant is brought forth, so through the joining of the creative forces of Spirit by souls attuned in love, the new body in Christ is speedily formed. The work can be done through individual effort, and there must always be continuous constructive action between the masculine and feminine faculties of soul and body; but the anointing with the precious love of the divine feminine is necessary to the great demonstration. The woman who anointed the head and feet of Jesus "loved much," and Jesus said that which she did would be remembered wherever the Gospel should be preached in the whole world. This symbolical representation of pouring into the masculine the pure love of the feminine is a guide for all women. All over the world the submerged love of the feminine is crying for release from the sensual dominance of the masculine. The remedy is: Anoint man's head (will) and his feet (understanding) with the Christ love, and he will be purified and satisfied. Not a word need be spoken to bring about the change. If in quietness and confidence the presence and the power of divine love are affirmed, the law will be fulfilled.

Love submerged in sense still retains the remembrance of her virginity and repels and resists the onslaughts of lust. Some of the most terrible ills are brought upon the body by the misuse of love. This is not the way of freedom; through a steady and firm holding to the one Presence and one Power will the son of man be lifted up, as Moses lifted up the serpent in the wilderness.

Wisdom and love combined are symbolically described in Scripture as the "Lamb slain from the foundation of the world" (KJV). But now men and women are studying the laws of Being and in some degree are striving to observe them in the marriage relation. Instead of submerging love in lust, the children of light retain their virgin purity and go hand in hand toward the dawn of a new order, in which there will be a bringing forth of the multitude of waiting souls in a way which is now hidden, but which will be revealed when love is lifted up.

> Call it not love, for love to heaven is fled
>   Since sweating lust on earth usurp'd his name;
> Under whose simple semblance he hath fed
>   Upon fresh beauty, blotting it with blame;
> Which the hot tyrant stains and soon bereaves,
> As caterpillars do the tender leaves.
>
> Love comforteth like sunshine after rain,
>   But lust's effect is tempest after sun;
> Love's gentle spring doth always fresh remain,
>   Lust's winter comes ere summer half be done;
> Love surfeits not, lust like a glutton dies;
> Love is all truth, lust full of forged lies.
>   —*Shakespeare*

CHAPTER 6

Power—Dominion—Mastery

Man does not exercise the power of his spiritual nature, because he lacks understanding of its character and of his relation to the originating Mind in which he exists. From Divine Mind man inherits power over the forces of his mind—in truth, power over all ideas. A quickening from on high must precede man's realization of his innate control of thought and feeling. The baptism of the Holy Spirit is a quickening of the spiritual nature, which is reflected in intellect and in body. When one understands the science of Being, one is prepared to receive this baptism and to utilize it along deeper lines of thought. Jesus had taught His apostles and followers, and they were prepared for the baptism that they received on the day of Pentecost.

"Ye shall receive power, when the Holy Spirit is come upon you." Power is essential to the work that Jesus Christ expects His followers to do in the great field of humanity. The command is: Go to every nation and preach the gospel. Man should apply the power of the word to his individual redemption, and he should speak the redeeming word of Spirit to the multitudinous thought people of his own soul and body.

Among the apostles of Jesus, Philip represents the power faculty of the mind. The word *Philip* means "a lover of horses." In physical activity the horse represents power; the ox, strength. Each of the twelve fundamental faculties of man has an ego that reflects, in a measure, the original man idea in God. In the body consciousness the Twelve Apostles, as egos, have twelve centers, or thrones, from which they exercise their power. The will expresses its dominion from the head; love, from the breast; and power (the ego whose character we are analyzing in this writing), from the throat. Power is one branch of the great tree; in Genesis it is named "life." The body of the life tree is the spinal cord, over which the motor system, with branches to every part of the organism, exercises its nervous energy.

The power center in the throat controls all the vibratory energies of the organism. It is the open door between the formless and the formed worlds of vibrations pertaining to the expression of sound. Every word that goes forth receives its specific character from the power faculty. When Jesus said, "The words that I have spoken unto you are spirit, and are life," He meant that through the spoken word He conveyed an inner spiritual quickening quality that would enter the mind of the recipient and awaken the inactive spirit and life. When the voice has united with the life of the soul, it takes on a sweetness and a depth that one feels and remembers; the voice that lacks this union is metallic and superficial. Voice culture may give one tone brilliancy, but every great singer has the soul contact. But higher and deeper still is the voice of one who has made union with Spirit and who can say with Jesus: "Heaven and earth shall pass away, but my words shall not pass away."

When we understand this power of the word, we have the key to the perpetuity of sacred writings. According to tradition, all the writings of the Bible were destroyed, but they were restored by Esdras, who, "remembered in his heart" and rewrote them. Modern discoveries in the realm of mind in a measure explain this mystical statement. We know now that every word that man utters makes an imprint in the astral ethers, and that, when there is consciousness of God life in the mind of the speaker, all his words become living identities and are perpetuated. Anyone who develops sufficient spiritual power may enter this book of life within the cosmic mind and read out of its pages.

The mind and the body of man have the power of transforming energy from one plane of consciousness to another. This is the power and dominion implanted in man from the beginning. According to Scripture, "God said, Let us make man in our image, after our likeness; and they shall have dominion over the fish of the sea, and over the fowl of the heaven, and over the cattle, and over all the earth, and over every creeping thing that creepeth upon the earth" (Gen. 1:26; Lesser translation). Paul cor-

roborates this statement by calling attention to the
glory of man's inheritance:

"Having the eyes of your heart enlightened, that ye may
know what is the hope of his calling, what the riches of the
glory of his inheritance in the saints, and what the exceeding
greatness of his power to usward who believe, according to that
working of the strength of his might which he wrought in
Christ, when he raised him from the dead, and made him to
sit at his right hand in the heavenly *places*, far above all rule,
and authority, and power, and dominion, and every name
that is named, not only in this world, but also in that which
is to come."

In the kingdom of God within man's consciousness, the power faculty plays an important part in
controlling the expression of the many emotions,
inspirations, and thoughts. The voice is the most
direct avenue of this expression, when man has
dominion over the emotions and feelings from
which the original impulse arises. The power of love
makes the voice rich, warm, and mellow. Man can
set love free in his soul by cultivating a loving attitude toward everybody and everything; he may add
strength by silently speaking words of strength to
each of the apostles sitting upon the twelve thrones
within. Power swings open all the doors of mind and
body. When one feels vital and energetic, the voice
is strong and vibrant and brilliant. When one is
sorrowful, the body weakens and the voice betrays
its lack by its mournful intonation. Through the vibrations of power in the throat, one can feel the
power of unity with the higher self more quickly
than in any other way. This reveals that ideas rule

the man; Jesus affirmed: "All power is given unto me in heaven [mind] and in earth [body]" (KJV). When Jesus made this affirmation He undoubtedly realized His innate spiritual dominion, and when He consciously attuned His spiritual identity to mind and body, there was a conscious influx of power, and His hearers said that He "taught them as having authority, and not as the scribes."

In the process of regeneration, the consciousness of power ebbs and flows, because the old and the new tides of thought act and react in the conscious and the subconscious realms of mind. However, when a disciple realizes his unity with Omnipotence, he is but little disturbed by the changes that go on in his mind and his body; he knows that his spiritual dominion is established, and that firm conviction expresses itself in firm words. Jesus said: "Heaven and earth shall pass away, but my words shall not pass away." Here is the evidence of spiritual power united with the idea of eternity. This union destroys the thought of years and declining power, and when awakened in those who have believed in age it will transform them and make all things new for them.

Every great vocalist has had inner spiritual power as an abiding conviction. This is strikingly illustrated in the indomitable persistency and power with which the famous singer Galli-Curci overcame obstacles. In the early stages of her career she was discouraged by opera critics. They told her that she could never make a success, but she persevered; and so she finally mastered every defect of her voice. This is a wonderful lesson to those who are apparently meeting with discouragements, who are tempted to succumb to circumstances and conditions in body and in environment. Take the words of Paul, "None of these things move me" (KJV), and make unqualified affirmations of your spiritual supremacy.

Some metaphysical schools warn their students against the development of power, because they fear that it will be used in selfish, ambitious ways. It doubtless is true that the personal ego sometimes lays hold of the power faculty and uses it for selfish aggrandizement; we can readily see how what is called the Devil had origin. To be successful in the use of the power of Being, one must be obedient in exercising all the ideas that make man. If there is an assumption of personal power, Lucifer falls like "lightning from heaven," and the adverse or carnal mind goes to and fro in the earth. The casting out of these demons of personality formed a large part of the work of Jesus, and those who follow Him in the regeneration are confronted with similar states of mind and find it necessary to cast out the great demon selfishness, which claims to have power but is a liar and the father of lies.

No disciple can do any great overcoming work without a certain realization of spiritual power, dominion, mastery. Without power, one easily gives up to temporal, [man-made] laws. The psychic atmosphere is filled with thoughts that are not in harmony with Divine Mind. These psychic thoughts are legion, and to overcome them one must be on one's guard. Jesus said, "Watch." This means that we should quicken our discernment and our ability to choose between the good and the evil. "And why even of yourselves judge ye not what is right?" This wisdom of Spirit is man's through the all-knowing and all-discerning power of Spirit within him, and he need never fear going wrong if he listens to his divine intuition. "Ye shall know the truth, and the truth shall make you free." But man can never be free until he declares his freedom. Jesus said "I am from above." It is the prerogative of every man to make this declaration and thereby rise above the psychisms [psychic constrictions] of mortal thought. Then do not fear to develop your power and mastery. They are not to be exercised on other people, but on yourself. "He that ruleth his spirit, [is more powerful] than he that taketh a city." Alexander cried because there were no more worlds to conquer, yet he had not conquered his own appetite, and died a drunkard at the age of thirty-three. Today men are striving to acquire power through money, legislation, and manmade government, and falling short because they have not mastered themselves.

Jesus said, "My kingdom is not of this world," yet He set up a kingdom in the world greater than all other kingdoms. In its beginning His kingdom was a very small affair, and the wise and the mighty laughed to scorn the proclamation that He was a king. Yet He was every inch a king. His people have been slow to follow the laws that He promulgated for His kingdom, but men in every walk of life are beginning to comprehend the vital integrity of His edicts. They are seeing that there can be no permanent peace or even civilization on earth until the Golden Rule, laid down by Him, is adopted by nations in commercial and in all other relationships. Businessmen are teaching the precept of Jesus, "All things therefore whatsoever ye would that men should do unto you, even so do ye also unto them," as fundamental in commercial success. Everywhere we hear them talking cooperation instead of competition. Commercial seers are discerning the dawn of a new day, in which good service instead of big profits will be the goal. Here we see the coming of the Christ "as a thief in the night." The night of ignorance and destructive competition is being burned out.

It follows that every kind of human industry must be carried forward by a power that recognizes the divine law. Man is the power of God in action. To man is given the highest power in the universe, the conscious power of thought. There is a universal creative force that urges man forward to a recognition of the creative power of his individual thought. This force is elemental, and all its attributes come under the dominion of man. When he cooperates with divine principle, man sits on the throne of his authority and the elemental force is subject to him.

But the power and the authority that are to rule in the kingdom of heaven are dependent on man's authority and his rule in the earth. Jesus said to Peter: "Whatsoever thou shalt bind on earth shall be bound in heaven; and whatsoever thou shalt loose on earth shall be loosed in heaven." If man binds or controls the appetites, passions, and emotions in the body (earth), he establishes ability and power to control the same forces in the realms universal, out of which the heavens are formed. When he attains a freedom in the expression of the qualities inherent in soul and body, he expands in power and can set free the elements universal and restore equilibrium between heaven and earth, or Spirit and matter.

When enough people have attained this power, the "new heaven and . . . new earth" (described in the twenty-first chapter of Revelation) will appear. It will not be necessary for anyone to wait for the full complement of overcomers, the mystical 144,000 who are to rule the new world, but each individual who complies with the overcoming law may enter into power with Jesus. It should not be overlooked by the elect that the Scripture reads: "He that overcometh shall inherit these things." To overcome and sit with Jesus on His throne means that man must overcome as He overcame. Jesus overcame the world, the flesh, and the Devil. To overcome the world one must be proof against all its allurements of riches and honor. To overcome the flesh one must spiritualize the five-sense man until material consciousness is raised to spiritual consciousness in feeling, tasting, seeing, hearing, and smelling. This change will ultimate in man's complete mastery of the body and in its final redemption from death.

The Devil is the personal ego who has in his freedom formed a state of consciousness peculiarly his own. When man lives wholly in the consciousness that personality has built up, he is ruled by the carnal mind, which is the Adversary, or Satan. In the mystery of the cross is hidden the overcoming of Satan. The crucifixion of Jesus is the symbolical representation of the crossing out (destruction) of the carnal mind (Satan) in the redeemed man's consciousness. Christ was not killed on the cross, neither was the body of Jesus destroyed. The "ghost" that Jesus gave up with His last breath was mortality. It was the personal, mortal consciousness that cried, "My God, my God, why hast thou forsaken me?" (The god should be spelled with a small *g*.) The personal-concept God fails to save its worshiper.

When the I AM identity, which is man, becomes so involved in its personal affairs that it ignores God, I AM lays hold of the body and rules all the bodily functions. When this rule is broken by the power of the Christ or supermind, there is a crucifixion. It may seem that Jesus is being crucified, but this is seeming only. Death comes to the Judas consciousness, which "hath a devil" (KJV), but the body, being closely connected with this usurping mind, passes through suffering and apparent death. This is no more than appearance, because the higher principle, the Christ, resurrects the body and transmutes it into higher spiritual substance, where it enters into harmony or heaven. The climax of man's power and dominion is set forth in the resurrection and ascension of the type man, Jesus.

CHAPTER 7

~~~~~

The Work of the Imagination in Regeneration

WHEN THE faculties of the mind are understood in their threefold relation—Spirit, soul, body—it will be found that every form and shape originated in the imagination. It is through the imagination that the formless takes form. It is well known that the artist sees in mind every picture that he puts on canvas. Man and the universe are a series of pictures in the Mind of Being. God made man in His image and likeness. Man, in his turn, is continually making and sending forth into his mind, his body, and the world about him living thought forms embodied and indued with his whole character. These images are formed in the front brain, and clothed with substance and life drawn from subcenters in the body.

Very intellectual people, concentrating the intensity of their thought in the head, fail to connect with the substance, life, and love centers in the body, and their work, although it may be very brilliant, lacks what we term "soul." The thought creations of this type seldom live long. Where the thought form and its substance are evenly balanced, the projected idea endures indefinitely. Jesus was a man thoroughly conversant with this law, and every idea that He clothed has lived and grown in wisdom and power in the minds of those who make union with Him in faith and spiritual understanding. He said: "Heaven and earth shall pass away: but my words shall not pass away."

Among the apostles, Bartholomew represents the imagination. He is called Nathanael in the first chapter of John, where it is recorded that Jesus saw him under the fig tree—the inference being that Jesus discerned Nathanael's presence before the latter came into visibility. This would indicate that images of people and things are projected into the imaging chamber of the mind and that by giving them attention one can understand their relation to outer things. Mind readers, clairvoyants, and dreamers have developed this capacity to a varying degree. Where consciousness is primary in soul unfoldment there is confusion, because of lack of understanding of the fundamental law of mind action. Forms are always manifestations of ideas. One who understands this can interpret the symbols shown to him in dreams and visions, but lack of understanding of this law makes one a psychic without power. Joseph was an interpreter because he sought the one creative Mind for guidance. "And Joseph answered Pharaoh, saying, It is not in me: God will give Pharaoh an answer of peace." When Pharaoh told him the dream about the fat kine and the lean kine, Joseph at once gave the real meaning of the dream; he understood the metaphysical law. The early Christians had understanding of this law. The same law is in existence today and can be used more effectually by us, the reincarnated followers of Jesus, because mind and its modes of action are now better understood.

The Spirit of Truth projects into the chamber of imagery pictures that, rightly understood, will be a sure guide for all people who believe in the omnipresence of Mind. Everybody dreams, but the great majority do not attempt to interpret the handwriting on the wall of the mind, or they take their dreams literally and, because the dreams do not come true, consider them foolish. Through ignorance of the law with which imagination works, man has made imagination a byword. We look upon imaginary things as trivial, yet we know that through the imagination we can produce wonderful changes in the body. Studying this law, we find that the character of both soul and body is determined by the imagination and its associated faculties. Paul referred to this power of the imagination when he wrote:

"But we all, with unveiled face beholding as in a mirror the glory of the Lord, are transformed into the same image from glory to glory, even as from the Lord the Spirit."

There has been much speculation about the method that Jesus used to impart spiritual understanding to His apostles and other early Christians, who were wonderfully illumined. It is true that the Twelve Apostles had His personal instruction, but it was apparently preparatory only; the thorough training was to follow. Jesus promised that the Spirit of Truth would, in His name, come as teacher, guide, and instructor. He did not say how Spirit would guide and teach those who believed in Him; we gain this conclusion from their experiences in the new school of life to which He introduced them.

It is possible to impart Truth through direct inspiration, but this requires a student with a development of mind superior to the average, and Jesus sought converts in every walk of life. So we find that the simple and universally intelligible avenue of visions and dreams, the work of the imagination, was adopted as an important means by which the believers were instructed and called together. In fact, a large part of the work of the early church was carried forward by this means.

Saul was converted by a vision. Jesus appeared to him in person and rebuked him for his persecution of the Christians, told him that He had a work for him to do, and gave him directions as to his future movements:

"And as he [Saul] journeyed, it came to pass that he drew nigh unto Damascus: and suddenly there shone round about him a light out of heaven: and he fell upon the earth, and heard a voice saying unto him, Saul, Saul, why persecutest thou me? And he said, Who art thou, Lord? And he said, I am Jesus whom thou persecutest; but rise, and enter into the city, and it shall be told thee what thou must do. And the men that journeyed with him stood speechless, hearing the voice, but beholding no man. And Saul arose from the earth; and when his eyes were opened, he saw nothing; and they led him by the hand, and brought him into Damascus. And he was three days without sight, and did neither eat nor drink."

Those who look to the Holy Spirit for guidance find that its instruction is given to all who believe in Christ, and they are often drawn together by direction of the inner voice, or by a dream, or by a vision. Saul, after beholding the blinding light of the spiritual realms, needed to have his sight restored. The brightness, or high potency, of Jesus' glorified presence had confused his intellectual consciousness, and this had brought about blindness. He needed the harmonious, peace-giving power of one who understood the inner life, and this was found in a certain disciple named Ananias. The Lord said to Ananias in a vision:

"Arise, and go to the street which is called Straight, and inquire in the house of Judas for one named Saul, a man of Tarsus: for behold, he prayeth; and he hath seen a man named Ananias coming in, and laying his hands on him, that he might receive his sight. But Ananias answered, Lord I have heard from many of this man, how much evil he did to thy saints at Jerusalem: and here he hath authority from the chief priests to bind all that call upon thy name. But the Lord said unto him, Go thy way: for he is a chosen vessel unto me, to bear my name before the Gentiles and kings, and the children of Israel: for I will show him how many things he must suffer for my name's sake. And Ananias departed, and entered into the house; and laying his hands on him said, Brother Saul, the Lord, even Jesus, who appeared unto thee in the way which thou camest, hath sent me, that thou mayest receive thy sight, and be filled with the Holy Spirit. And straightway there

fell from his eyes as it were scales, and he received his
sight; and he arose and was baptized; and he took food and
was strengthened."

The Lord's appearing to Saul, with the conversion of the latter, is considered one of the great
miracles of the Bible, but the experience of Ananias
is seldom mentioned. Yet we are told in this text
that the Lord appeared to Ananias and talked to
him, just as He had appeared and talked to Saul,
and there was apparently no difference in the real
character of the incidents, except such be found in
the mental attitude of the participants. Saul was
antagonistic and full of fight. Ananias was receptive
and obedient; he doubtless had received this sort of
guidance many times. From the text we readily
discern his spiritual harmony. He knew the reputa-
tion of Saul and protested against meeting him,
but the Lord explained the situation and Ananias
obeyed.

Today disciples of Jesus who are obedient and
receptive and believe in the presence and the power
of the Master and the Holy Spirit are everywhere
receiving visions and dreams. They are being drawn
together and are helping one another to recover
from the discords and inharmonies of life. Never
before in the history of the race has there been so
great a need for spiritual instruction as there is now,
and this need is being met by Jesus and His aids in
a renaissance of early Christianity and of its methods
of instruction.

Spirit imparts its ideas through a universal language. Instead of being explained by words and phrases as used in ordinary language, the idea is formed and projected in its original character. This system of transferring intelligence is called symbolism. It is the only universal and correct means of communicating ideas. For example, if one wished to tell about a procession that he had seen, and could mentally picture it so that others could see it, how much more complete the communication than descriptive words! The mind formulates into thought images every idea that arises in it, and then tries to express it in language, which is nearly always inadequate. The French say: "Words are employed to conceal ideas." As the early disciples of Jesus had to learn that the symbol represents the idea rather than the thing, so modern disciples, following the same line of instruction, should not allow the intellect to materialize their dreams and visions; although they may be puzzled, like Peter, subsequent events will bring to them a clearer understanding of the lesson.

In the tenth chapter of Acts, we read:

"Peter went up upon the housetop to pray, about the sixth hour: and he became hungry, and desired to eat: but while they made ready, he fell into a trance; and he beholdeth the heaven opened, and a certain vessel descending, as it were a great sheet, let down by four corners upon the earth: wherein were all manner of four-footed beasts and creeping things of the earth and birds of the heaven. And there came a voice to him, Rise, Peter;

kill and eat. But Peter said, Not so, Lord; for I have never
eaten anything that is common and unclean. And a voice
came unto him again the second time, What God hath
cleansed, make not thou common. And this was done
thrice: and straightway the vessel was received up into
heaven.

"Now while Peter was much perplexed in himself what
the vision which he had seen might mean, behold, the men
that were sent by Cornelius, having made inquiry for
Simon's house, stood before the gate, and called and asked
whether Simon, who was surnamed Peter, were lodging
there. And while Peter thought on the vision, the Spirit
said unto him, Behold, three men seek thee."

Peter was still bound by the Jewish teaching
that there was no salvation for any except those of
his faith, and this vision was to break the bondage
of such narrowness and show him that the gospel
of Jesus Christ is for all people. In a vision the
Lord had already instructed Cornelius, the Roman
soldier, that he should send certain of his servants
to Joppa and fetch Peter to Caesarea.

Some advocates of flesh eating make the mistake
of giving a literal interpretation to Peter's vision,
holding that the Lord commanded him to kill and
eat "all manner of fourfooted beasts and creeping
things of the earth and birds of the heaven" and
that God has cleansed them and thus prepared them
for food for man. If this view of the vision should
be carried out literally, we should eat all four-
footed animals, including skunks, all the creeping
things, and all birds of the air, including vultures.
We know, however, that the vision is to be taken

in its symbolizing meaning. Peter was to appropriate and harmonize in his inner consciousness all thoughts of separation, all uncleanliness and impurity, narrowness, selfishness—the thoughts that bring diversity and separation.

We have within us, bound in the cage of the subconsciousness, all the propensities and the savagery of the animals. In the regeneration these are brought forth and a great reconciliation takes place. We find that there is really nothing unclean, except to human consciousness. In the original creative idealism of Divine Mind, everything was made perfect and sanctified and pronounced "very good." But God did not tell man to eat everything because it was good in its place.

"And God said, Behold, I have given you every herb yielding seed, which is upon the face of all the earth, and every tree, in which is the fruit of a tree yielding seed; to you it shall be for food."

When man has regenerated and lifted up the beasts of the field, he will carry out the injunction given to the original Adam and name them "good."

Man's body represents the sum total of the animal world, because in its evolution it has had experience in nearly every type of elemental form. These memories are part of the soul, and in the unregenerate they come to the surface sporadically. Sometimes whole nations seem to revert from culture to savagery without apparent cause, but there is always a cause. These reversions are the result of some violent wrenching of the soul, or of concentration, to the exclusion of everything else, on a line of thought out of harmony with divine law. When the soul is ready for its next step in the upward way, a great change takes place, known as regeneration. Jesus referred to this when He said to Nicodemus, "Ye must be born anew." In one of its phases the new birth is a resurrection. All that man has passed through has left its image in the subconsciousness, wrought in mind and matter. These images are set free in the regeneration, and man sees them as part of himself. In his *Journal*, George Fox, the spiritual-minded Quaker, says:

I was under great temptations sometimes, and my inward sufferings were heavy; but I could find none to open my condition to but the Lord alone, unto whom I cried night and day. I went back into Nottinghamshire, where the Lord shewed me that the natures of those things which were hurtful without, were within the hearts and minds of wicked men. The natures of dogs, swine, vipers, of Sodom and Egypt, Pharaoh, Cain, Ishmael, Esau, etc. The natures of these I saw within, though people had been looking without. I cried to the Lord saying, "Why should I be thus, seeing I was never addicted to commit those evils?" And the Lord answered, "It was needful I should have a sense of all conditions, how else should I speak of all conditions?" In this I saw the infinite love of God. I saw also, that there was an ocean of darkness and death; but an infinite ocean of light and love, which flowed over the ocean of darkness. In that also I saw the infinite love of God, and I had great openings. As I was walking by the steeple-house side in the town of Mansfield, the Lord said unto me, "That which people trample upon must be thy food." And as the Lord spake he opened to me that people and professors trampled upon the life, even the life of Christ was trampled upon; they fed upon words, and fed one another with words; but trampled under foot the blood of the son of God, which blood was my life: and they lived in their airy notions talking of him. It seemed strange to me at the first, that I should feed on that which the high professors trampled upon; but the Lord opened it clearly to me by his eternal Spirit and power.

In the regeneration man finds that he has, in the part of his soul called the natural man, animal propensities corresponding to the animals in the outer world. In the pictures of the mind, these take form as lions, horses, oxen, dogs, cats, snakes, and the birds of the air. The visions of Joseph, Daniel, John, and other Bible seers were of this character. When man understands that these animals represent thoughts, working in the subconsciousness, he has a key to the many causes of bodily conditions. It is clear to him that the prophets of old were using symbols to express ideas, and he sees that to interpret these symbols he must learn what each represents, in order to get the original meaning.

According to Genesis, the original creation was ideal, and through man the ideal was given character and form. Adam gave character to all the beasts of the field: "And whatever the man called every living creature, that was the name thereof." To the spiritually wise it is revealed that, when man is fully redeemed, he redeems and purifies and uplifts the animals in himself. The animal world will go through a complete transformation when the race is redeemed. As Isaiah says, "The wolf and the lamb shall feed together, and the lion shall eat straw like the ox." Some even go farther than this, and say that in the millennium there will be no necessity for animals; that they are, in reality, the dissipated forces of the human family and that when those forces are finally gathered into the original fount in the subjective, there will be no more animals in the objective; that in this way man will be immensely strengthened and a certain connection will be made between the so-called material and the spiritual.

CHAPTER 8

Understanding

REFERENCE to the dictionary shows the words *wisdom, understanding, knowledge,* and *intelligence* to be so closely related that their definitions overlap in a most confusing way. The words differ in meaning, but various writers on the mind and its faculties have given definitions of these words in terms that directly oppose the definitions of other writers. There are two schools of writers on metaphysical subjects, and their definitions are likely to confuse a student unless he knows to which class the writer belongs. First are those who handle the mind and its faculties from an intellectual standpoint, among whom may be mentioned Kant, Hegel, Mill, Schopenhauer, and Sir William Hamilton. The other school includes all the great company of religious authors who have discerned that Spirit and soul are the causing factors of the mind. Compilers of dictionaries have consulted the former class for their definitions, and we have in consequence an inadequate set of terms to express the deep things of the mind. Even Christian metaphysicians who belong in the second classification have no clear understanding of the two great realms of mind: first, that in which pure ideas and pure logic rule; and second, the realm in which the

thoughts and the actions of the mind are concerned
with reason and the relation of ideas in the outer
world. It is only in the last half-century that large
numbers of Christians have discerned that Jesus
taught a metaphysical science.

Poets are natural mystics and metaphysicians,
and in their writings we find the safest definitions of
the names used to represent the actions of the mind.
Poets nearly always make the proper distinction
between wisdom and understanding. Tennyson says,
"Knowledge comes, but wisdom lingers." Spiritual
discernment always places wisdom above the other
faculties of mind and reveals that knowledge and intelligence are auxiliary to understanding. Intellectual understanding comes first in the soul's development, then a deeper understanding of principles
follows, until the whole man ripens into wisdom.

"'Tis the sunset of life gives me mystical lore,
    And coming events cast their shadows before."

The writings of the Hebrew prophets are good
examples of original inspiration, which is wisdom.
Solomon was famous for his wisdom. Jehovah appeared to him in a dream and said: "Ask what I
shall give thee." Solomon replied: "Give thy servant
therefore an understanding heart to judge thy people, that I may discern between good and evil."
Pleased because Solomon had asked for wisdom instead of riches and honor, the Lord said:

"Behold, I have done according to thy word, lo I have
given thee a wise and an understanding heart . . . . And I

have also given thee that which thou hast not asked, both
riches and honor . . . . And Solomon awoke; and, behold, it
was a dream."

It was after this occurrence that two women appealed to Solomon to decide which of them really
was the mother of the child that they both claimed.

"And the king said, Fetch me a sword. . . . And the
king said, Divide the living child in two, and give half to
the one, and half to the other. Then spake the woman
whose the living child was unto the king, for her heart
yearned over her son, and she said, Oh, my lord give her
the living child, and in no wise slay it. But the other
said, It shall be neither mine nor thine; divide it. Then the
king answered and said, Give her the living child, and in no
wise slay it: she is the mother thereof. And all Israel heard
of the judgment which the king had judged; and they
feared the king: for they saw that the wisdom of God was
in him, to do justice."

The foregoing is a fine example of intuitive
knowing. Instead of indulging in the usual taking
of testimony and the various methods of proving
the case by witnesses, Solomon appealed directly to
the heart and got the truth quickly. No amount of
exoteric testimony would have accomplished what
the appeal to love brought forth at once.

Although it is sometimes difficult to determine
between pure knowing and the quick perception of
the intellect, the decision can always be made truly,
based on the presence of the affectional nature.

Great philosophers in every age have testified to
the activity of a supermind quality, which they have

variously named. Socrates had it. He called it his "daemon." Plato named it "pure reason." Jesus called it the "kingdom of the heavens."

In an article by M. K. Wisehart printed in the *American Magazine* for June 1930 and entitled "A Close Look at the World's Greatest Thinker," Professor Albert Einstein is quoted as saying:

"'Every man knows that in his work he does best and accomplishes most when he has attained a proficiency that enables him to work intuitively. That is, there are things which we come to know so well that we do not know how we know them. So it seems to me in matters of principle. Perhaps we live best and do things best when we are not too conscious of how and why we do them.'

"He spoke of the great extent to which intuition figures in his work, and gave me to understand that the ability to work by intuition is one that can be acquired in any walk of life. It comes as the result of prolonged effort and reflection and application and failures and trying again. Then, in the end, one knows things without knowing how one knows them! And I gathered that the Professor meant to say that no man knows anything until he knows it in this thorough, instinctive way.

"People frequently ask Professor Einstein whether, as a scientist, he believes in God. Usually he answers: 'I do not believe in a God who maliciously or arbitrarily interferes in the personal affairs of mankind. My religion consists of an humble admiration for the vast power which manifests itself in that small part of the universe which our poor, weak minds can grasp!'

"In a discussion, when the Professor is impressed by the correctness of his own views or those of another, he will suddenly exclaim: 'Yes! So it is! It is just! It must be so! I am quite sure that God could not have made it different!' For him, God is as valid as a scientific argument.

"At one time, after prolonged concentration upon a single problem (it lasted for nearly four years), the Professor suffered a complete physical collapse. With it came severe stomach trouble. A celebrated specialist said: 'You must not get out of bed! You cannot stand on your feet for a long time to come.'

"'Is this the will of God?' queried the Professor instantly. 'I think not! The voice of God is from within us. Something within me tells me that every day I must get up at least once. I must go to the piano and play! The rest of the day I will spend in bed! This I am prepared to accept as the will of God!'

"And with the will of God, as set forth by Einstein, the specialist had to be content. Every day the Professor got up, put his bathrobe over his night-shirt, and went to the piano to play.

"I asked many questions to elicit the lessons of his experience that might be of most use to the rest of us. I learned that he reads little. 'Much reading after a certain age,' he says, 'diverts the mind from its creative pursuits. Any man who reads too much and uses his own brain too little falls into lazy habits of thinking, just as the man who spends too much time in the theaters is apt to be content with living vicariously instead of living his own life.

"'I have only two rules which I regard as principles of conduct. The first is: Have no rules. The second is: Be independent of the opinion of others.'"

So we find that there is in man a knowing capacity transcending intellectual knowledge. Nearly everyone has at some time touched this hidden wisdom and has been more or less astonished at its revelations. It certainly is a most startling experience to find ourselves giving forth logical thoughts and words without preparation or forethought, because we nearly always arrive at our conclusions through a process of reasoning. However, the reasoning process is often so swift that we are likely to think that it is true inspiration, especially when we have received either the reflected uplift of other wise ones or the baptism of the Holy Spirit. This quickening of the intellect is the John-the-Baptist or intellectual illumination that precedes the awakening of the ideal, the Christ understanding. Some Truth students become so enamored of the revelations that they receive through the head that they fail to go on to the unfoldment of the One who baptizes in "Holy Spirit and in fire." The Old Testament writers had a certain understanding of the first and the second opening of the mind to spiritual Truth; Isaiah said:

"The voice of one that crieth, Prepare ye in the wilderness the way of Jehovah; make level in the desert a high way for our God."

Elijah had intellectual illumination, and the Israelites were taught that he would come again as a forerunner of the Messiah. Jesus said that Elijah had come again in the personality of John the Baptist:

"I say unto you, that Elijah is come already, and they knew him not . . . Then understood the disciples that he spake unto them of John the Baptist."

The history of the Israelites is a sort of moving picture of man's soul and body development. When we understand the psychology of the different scenes, we know what we have passed through or will pass through in our journey from sense to Spirit.

Intellectual understanding of Truth, as given in the first baptism, is a tremendous step in advance of sense consciousness, and its possession brings a temptation to use for selfish ends the wisdom and the power thereby revealed. When Jesus received this baptism He was "led up of the Spirit into the wilderness to be tempted of the devil" (personal ego) before he could take the next degree in Son-of-God consciousness.

But Jesus knew that the illumination of the personal is not the fulfillment of the law, and He rejected every temptation to use His understanding for selfish ends.

Unless the disciple is very meek he will find the mortal ego strongly asserting its arguments for the application of the power of Spirit to personal needs. The god of mammon is bidding high for men that have received the baptism of Spirit, and many sell out, but their end is dust and ashes. No man can serve two masters; one cannot serve both God and Mammon.

When we discover in ourselves a flow of thought that seems to have been evolved independently of the reasoning process, we are often puzzled about its origin and its safety as a guide. In its beginnings this seemingly strange source of knowledge is often turned aside as a daydream; again it seems a distant voice, an echo of something that we have heard and forgotten. One should give attention to this un-usual and usually faint whispering of Spirit in man. It is not of the intellect and it does not originate in the skull. It is the development, in man, of a greater capacity to know himself and to understand the purpose of creation. The Bible gives many ex-amples of the awakening of this brain of the heart in seers, in lawgivers, and in prophets. It is accredited as coming from the heart. The nature of the process is not explained; one who is in the devotional stage of unfoldment need not know all the complex movements of the mind in order to get the message of the Lord. It is enough to know that the under-standing is opened in both head and heart when man gives himself wholly to the Lord.

This relation of head and heart is illustrated in the lives of John the Baptist and Jesus. They were cousins; the understanding of the head bears a close relation to the wisdom of the heart. They both re-ceived the baptism of Spirit, John preceding Jesus and baptizing Him. Here the natural order of spiritual illumination is illustrated. Man receives first an intellectual understanding of Truth which he transmits to his heart, where love is awakened. The Lord reveals to him that the faculty of love is the greatest of all the powers of man and that head knowledge must decrease as heart understanding increases.

However, we should remember that none of the faculties is eliminated in the regeneration. Among the apostles of Jesus, Thomas typifies the head, representing reason and intellectual perception. Jesus did not ignore Thomas's demand for physical evidence of His identity, but respected it. He convinced Thomas by corporal evidence that there had been a body resurrection; that He was living, not in a physical [psychical] or ghost body, but in the same body that had been crucified.

Jesus plainly taught that He had attained control of the life in the body and could take it up or lay it down. We may construe the death and the resurrection of Jesus in various ways, many of them fanciful and allegorically far removed from practical life, but the fact remains that there is good historical evidence of the physical reality of the Resurrection in its minutest detail.

Spiritual understanding shows us that the resurrection of the body from death is not to be confined to Jesus, but is for all men who comprehend Truth and apply it as Jesus applied it. He had the consciousness of the new flood of life that comes to all who open their minds and their bodies to the living

Word of God, and He knew that it would raise the atomic vibration of His organism above the disintegrating thought currents of the earth and thus would save His flesh from corruption.

When Jesus told the Jews what He discerned, they said that He was crazy ("hath a demon"). One who teaches and practices the higher understanding and reality of man's relation to the creative law is not sane—from the viewpoint of mortal man.

When the higher understanding in Jesus proclaimed, "Verily, verily, I say unto you, If a man keep my word, he shall never see death," they took up stones to cast at Him. This startling claim of the power of the word of Truth to save one from death is beyond all human reason, and it is resented by the material thoughts, which are as hard as rocks.

Jesus did not let the limited race thought about man keep Him from doing the works of Spirit. He knew that the light of Truth had arisen in His consciousness, and He was not afraid to affirm it. He went right ahead healing the sick and teaching the Truth as He saw it, regardless of the traditions of the Hebrew fathers, Abraham, Isaac, and Jacob. He kept the light shining in His consciousness by being loyal to it and by making for Himself the highest statements of Truth that He could conceive. The Christ Mind speaking in Him said: "I am the light of the world."

Spiritual understanding is developed in a multitude of ways; no two persons have exactly the same experience. One may be a Saul, to whom the light comes in a blinding flash, while to another the light may come gently and harmoniously. The sudden breaking forth of the light indicates the existence of stored-up reservoirs of spiritual experience, gained from previous lives. Jesus saw that Saul had a spiritual capacity that, turned into right channels, would do great good; so He took some pains to awaken in Saul the true light and thereby restrain the destructive zeal that possessed him. "He is a chosen vessel unto me, to bear my name before the Gentiles and kings, and the children of Israel."

The spiritual nature develops in man as the other attributes of his character develop. "As he thinketh within himself, so is he" is a statement of the law that has no exception. Man develops the capacity to do that which he sets out to do. If one makes no start one never goes.

> In idle wishes fools supinely stay;
> Be there a will, then wisdom finds a way.

No one ever attained spiritual consciousness without striving for it. The first step is to ask. "Ask, and it shall be given you; seek, and ye shall find; knock, and it shall be opened unto you." Prayer is one form of asking, seeking, and knocking. Then make your mind receptive to the higher understanding, through silent meditations and affirmations of Truth. The earnest desire to understand spiritual things will open the way, and revelation within and without will follow. In Daniel 10:12 it is written:

"Fear not, Daniel; for from the first day that thou didst set thy heart to understand, and to humble thyself before thy God, thy words were heard: and I am come for thy words' sake."

Daniel humbled himself in the presence of the universal Mind, and thereby opened his understanding and made himself receptive to the cosmic consciousness. Daniel and his companions were superior in wisdom and understanding to all the native magicians and seers in the whole Babylonian realm. The Scriptures say that God gave Daniel knowledge and skill in all learning and wisdom, and "Daniel had understanding in all visions and dreams." Cultivate purity of mind and body, and you will open the way for the higher thoughts, as did Daniel. He "purposed in his heart that he would not defile himself with the king's dainties, nor with the wine which he drank: therefore he requested of the prince of the eunuchs that he might not defile himself."

Spiritual understanding is developed in the feminine realm of the soul. This development is pictured in Acts 16:14: "And a certain woman named Lydia, a seller of purple, of the city of Thyatira, one that worshipped God, heard us: whose heart the Lord opened."

Thyatira means "burning incense"; it represents the intense desire of man for the higher expressions of life. When this inner urge comes forth with power (seller of purple), the Lord opens the heart and we receive the heavenly message, like the disciples who said one to another, "Was not our heart burning within us, while he spake to us in the way, while he opened to us the scriptures?"

"Wisdom consisteth not in knowing many things, nor even in knowing them thoroughly; but in choosing and in following what conduces the most certainly to our lasting happiness and true glory." —*Landor*

"Knowledge dwells in heads replete with thoughts of other men, wisdom in minds attentive to their own." —*Cowper*

"She [knowledge] is earthly of the mind, but wisdom heavenly of the soul." —*Tennyson*

"Create in me a clean heart, O God;
And renew a right spirit within me."
—*Psalm 51:10*

"For wisdom shall enter into thy heart,
And knowledge shall be pleasant unto thy soul."
—*Proverbs 2:10*

"But the path of the righteous is as the dawning light,
That shineth more and more unto the perfect day."
—*Proverbs 4:18*

"A tranquil heart is the life of the flesh;
But envy is the rottenness of the bones."
—*Proverbs 14:30*

"My son, forget not my law;
But let thy heart keep my commandments."
—*Proverbs 3:1*

"Trust in Jehovah with all thy heart,
And lean not upon thine own understanding:
In all thy ways acknowledge him,
And he will direct thy paths."
—*Proverbs 3:5-6*

"Happy is the man that findeth wisdom,
 And the man that getteth understanding.
 For the gaining of it is better than the gaining of silver,
 And the profit thereof than fine gold.
 She is more precious than rubies:
 And none of the things thou canst desire are to be
         compared unto her.
 Length of days is in her right hand;
 In her left hand are riches and honor.
 Her ways are ways of pleasantness,
 And all her paths are peace.
 She is a tree of life to them that lay hold upon her:
 And happy is every one that retaineth her.
 Jehovah by wisdom founded the earth;
 By understanding he established the heavens."

—Proverbs 3:13-19

CHAPTER 9

The Will Is the Man

Our caption is quoted from an ancient metaphysical teaching, the origin of which is lost in antiquity. The idea is that the development of the will is possible only through the development of the mind as a whole, and as man is mind, "the will is the man." This conclusion is reached because the will moves to action all the other faculties of the mind and seems to be the whole process.

However, a careful analysis of the various factors entering into an action reveals other equally important attributes of man, and we cannot wholly admit that "the will is the man." The will is undoubtedly the focal point around which all action centers, when there is harmony of mind; but the rule has been accepted by schools of philosophy from most ancient times down to the present that the will and the understanding are very closely related —the understanding comprehending all our speculative, the will all our active powers. This close relationship is symbolically taught in the Bible, and it appeals to man's reason and is confirmed by his observation.

Jacob, representing the I AM (I will be what I will to be), had twelve sons, one of whom was Joseph, "the dreamer." Joseph represents the imag-

97

ination, by which all forms and shapes are brought
into manifestation. In the development of the mind,
certain faculties are given prominence. After they
run their race, other faculties that have been held
in reserve come forward. When the period of rest
comes, the Scriptures recite that a certain one "died,
old and full of days." As man goes forward in his
unfoldment, there is sometimes a tendency toward
the surface of consciousness, or the phenomenal,
and a gradual loss of interest in the original sources
of action. The phenomenal phase of creation is so interesting that man sometimes becomes bewildered
in its study or its pleasure, and the originating
cause may be ignored to the point of forgetfulness.
This cessation of creative activity by the imagination (Joseph) is described in these words: "So
Joseph died, being a hundred and ten years old: and
they embalmed him, and he was put in a coffin in
Egypt." This means metaphysically that when the
imagination in a life span has fulfilled its mission as
a creative power it falls asleep, but it is preserved in
the realm of darkness (Egypt).

Joseph's number is eleven. He was the eleventh
son, and his age when he stopped active work and
fell asleep (110) represents the completeness of the
dispensation of that faculty's activity; the cipher
indicates an endless capacity for expression. The
figure given as the age of a Biblical character usually
represents the subject's place in his evolution. Joseph
completed his evolution to the eleventh degree plus.
The cipher means that he has more to demonstrate.

Jesus' number is twelve. He was wise at the age of twelve.

Adam was third in the Godhead (God, Christ, man). He lived 930 years, according to scriptural chronology. This number tells us that he is third in the trinity, has the capacity of the twelvefold man, but has unfolded only three of the twelve faculties. The order of the numbers indicates the harmony of his unfoldment. In this instance it was orderly—the naught denotes future progress uninterrupted.

Seth, the son whom Adam begat "in his own likeness, after his image," represents the awakening of spiritual consciousness. "Then began men to call upon the name of Jehovah." Seth's years were 912. Here the trinity and the twelvefold man are epitomized, and we see that Seth was the birth, in Adam, of Adam's own original character, even the image and likeness of Elohim. In the figure nine the trinity is repeated three times, once for each of its identities: God, Christ, man; then the twelve powers of man are added. Again the total of the digits is twelve, the number of divine man demonstrated.

We have called attention to the metaphysical meaning of the chronology of these Biblical characters in order to illustrate more fully the manner in which the faculties are developed. It will be seen that in man is implanted the likeness of God, which man develops in a long series of personalities. The process of forming a soul may be compared to the development, in a photographic negative, of the image that has been imprinted upon the sensitive plate but cannot be seen until it has been put through a regular developing process. When Adam had a spiritual awakening he perceived the Truth of his identity in God, and thereby begat Seth, the original image and likeness of spiritual man, imprinted upon him by the Word of creative Mind. Then the worship of Jehovah was restored in man's whole consciousness, for a time at least.

Coming down the chronological stream, we find that Joseph's place was taken by two sons. "And Joseph called the name of the first-born Manasseh: For, *said he,* God hath made me forget all my toil, and all my father's house. And the name of the second called he Ephraim: For God hath made me fruitful in the land of my affliction." The mother of these sons was Asenath, daughter of Potiphera, Egyptian priest of On. Asenath means "peril." She represents the feminine or love side of the natural man. From this intricate symbology we discern that two faculties of the mind were given birth. The eldest son, Manasseh, had power to forget, to erase by denial, through an understanding of Truth, all the accumulated burden of thoughts, even to that of heredity, "all my father's house." The other son, Ephraim, could add to by affirmation and make fruitful the land that seemed to be a place of affliction. These two sons of Joseph inherited his allotment in the Promised Land, which symbolizes the perfected body. The front brain is the field of operation for these closely related faculties—imagination, understanding, and will. When man's will is working strongly he corrugates his brow, and his quick understanding causes his eyes to flash.

When the imagination is subjective and spiritual and the will and the understanding are objective and alert, we have the creative artist. Then the understanding develops its greatest freedom and originality. It is no longer bound by the traditions of the past in literature, art, music, drama, science, or religion, but launches out into the deep and brings up the "pearl of great price," original creative genius and life. Then the energetic will makes fruitful by its activity all the inspirations of the awakened man.

These two closely related forces of the mind are dominant in the race because their practicality is necessary in man's free development. If the imagination were wholly in command, it would eventually run into a riot of daydreams or fanciful schemes that could not be worked out successfully in a world where natural law is inexorable. It is this "peril" (Asenath) that the mind considers, and brings forth, in sequence, will and understanding. "The highest and most excellent thing in man," says Goethe, "is formless, and we must guard against giving it shape in anything save noble deeds."

Man is a free agent in the possession and the use of the faculty of will. Freedom of will has been variously regarded and defined. It is the subject of volumes of theological literature and also the rock on which religionists have split. The theory of predestination relieves man of all responsibility. If

God has fixed every act of man's existence, then there can be no mental or moral freedom. If man cannot determine the character of his acts, he has neither understanding nor will—he is a puppet.

The understanding and the will should be especially active in one who would master the sensations of the body. Potiphar's wife represents the sense consciousness that tempts us to meet its desires and, when we deny it, has us imprisoned. This means that when a certain habit in the sense consciousness is refused expression, it reacts and for a time seems to prevent our expressing even the good. But let us patiently bide our time; the higher will yet show its God-given power.

The several visits of Joseph's brothers to Egypt for corn, and the final reconciliation, are symbolical representations of the manner in which we make connection with the obscured vitality within the organism and finally bring all our faculties into conjunction with it.

Volumes might be written with Joseph as a text. In his history, as given in Genesis, some of the most interesting processes of regeneration are symbolized. This hidden realm within the subconsciousness is in an Egyptian, or obscured, state to most of us. Yet it is a great kingdom, and its king is Pharaoh, ruler of the sun, or the "brain" and nerve center, which physiology names the solar plexus. This is the "brain" of the physical man, and it directs the circulation, digestion, assimilation, and so forth. Students of mind have discovered that the solar plexus is the organ through which a ruling thought in the head is carried into the body. He of the "hard heart," who would not let the people go, is human will, acting through the solar plexus, or city of the sun.

The spiritual life in the subconsciousness (Children of Israel in Egypt) is often prevented from expressing itself by the opposition of the will. If the understanding decides that what it conceives to be the natural law shall be the limit of expression, there is further bondage and there are harder tasks. Any hard, dictatorial, or willful state of mind will harden the heart. This state of mind acts through the solar plexus (the distributing station for building forces of the body), and thereby brings its limitations upon the whole system. Hardened arteries are the result of hard thoughts; this hardness originates in the will. Jehovah represents the law of the I AM in action.

The ambiguity in the term *motive* has caused much of the controversy that has raged over free will. The champions of free will commonly suppose that before performing an act a man is affected by various motives, none of which necessarily determines his act. Their opponents, on the other hand, argue that there is no such thing as this unmotivated choice. Some hold that free will proper consists of choice only as between higher and lower good. Some regard it as consisting in the power to do as one pleases or chooses. Others define it as the power to do or to choose as one should.

According to some academic metaphysicians, the freedom of the will includes the power to act contrary to all of one's own motives or inclinations or tendencies, this power being inherent in the will. It is readily seen that this thing called "motive" is another name for understanding, and that it is a necessary adjunct to that faculty. But not all people use understanding as the headlight for both motive and will. The undisciplined mind feels the impulse that lies behind motive and acts without considering either cause or effect. This is partaking of the knowledge of good and evil without heeding the voice of wisdom—the sin of Adam, undeveloped man. Understanding may be illumined by the Christ Mind, and thus receive the light that "lighteth every man, coming into the world." Without this light man breaks the law in nearly every act. The divorcement of understanding from will has led to endless controversies between those who have written and debated about the necessity for man's having free will, and those who, because of the evils that have come upon man through ignorant willing, have advocated the utter effacement of the will.

We do not need less will; we need more understanding. Jesus (spiritual light) showed Thomas (intellectual understanding) the wounds that ignorance had inflicted upon the innocent body. Jesus' apostles represented His own faculties of mind. When He called them they were ignorant and undisciplined children of the natural world. But the image and likeness of the creative Mind was on them, to discipline them in the wisdom of the Christ (spiritual I AM).

As the executive power of the mind, human will is the negative pole of spiritual decision. Right here is where those who study man from a personal viewpoint fail in their estimate of his power and his accountability. As mortal, living in a material world, he seems circumscribed and limited in capacity and destiny. Philosophers have studied man in this cage of the mind, and their conclusions have been that he is little better than a reasoning animal.

But there is a higher and truer estimate of man, and that estimate is made from what the academic school of philosophy would call the purely speculative side of existence. Failing to discern his spiritual origin, they fail in estimating his real character. As a product of the natural man, will is often a destructive force. Nearly all our systems of training children have been based on breaking the will in order to gain authority over the child and obedience from him. We should remember that the right to exercise freedom of will was given to man in the beginning, according to Genesis, and that will should always be given its original power and liberty.

It is possible, however, for man so to identify his consciousness with Divine Mind that he is moved in every thought and act by that Mind. Jesus attained this unity; when He realized that He was willing not in the personal but in the divine, He said: "Not my will, but thine, be done."

Many sincere Christians have tried to follow in the way of Jesus, and they have negatively submitted their will to God. But they have not attained

the power or the authority of Jesus by so doing.
The reason is that they have not raised their will to
the positive spiritual degree. Jesus was not negative
in any of His faculties, and He did not teach a doctrine of submission. He gave, to those who went
forth preaching the Gospel, the power and authority of the Holy Spirit. In Mark 16:16-18 it is
recorded that Jesus says: "He that believeth and is
baptized shall be saved; but he that disbelieveth
shall be condemned. And these signs shall accompany them that believe: in my name shall they cast
out demons; they shall speak with new tongues;
they shall take up serpents, and if they drink any
deadly thing, it shall in no wise hurt them; they
shall lay hands on the sick, and they shall recover."
We must believe in the higher powers and be immersed in the omnipresent water of life. If we fail to
exercise faith in things spiritual, we are condemned
to the prison of materiality.

Some Christians believe that God's will toward
men varies, that His will changes, that He chastises
the disobedient and punishes the wicked. This
view of God's character is gained from the Old Testament. Jehovah was the tribal God of the Israelites
as Baal was of the Philistines. Men's concepts of
God are measured by their spiritual understanding. The Jehovah, of Moses, is quite different from
the Father, of Jesus, yet they are spiritually one and
the same. "It is not the will of your Father who is in
heaven, that one of these little ones should perish,"
is the teaching of Jesus. He bore witness that

the will of God is that men should not suffer—that through Him they should have complete escape from sin, sickness, and even death. "God so loved the world, that he gave his only begotten Son, that whosoever believeth on him should not perish, but have eternal life." The sin, sickness, suffering, and death that men experience are not punishment willed by God; they are results of broken law. The law is good; men have joy, satisfaction, and life in everlasting harmony, when they keep the law. Creation would not be possible without rules governing the created.

It is error for anyone to submit his will to the control of any personality. The personal exercise of will by personal understanding is shortsighted and selfish; hence it is never safe to allow oneself to be led by the direction or advice of another. Practice the presence of God until you open your consciousness to the inflow of the omnipresent, all-knowing mind, then affirm your unity with that mind until you know and fully realize, through the many avenues of wisdom, just what you should do. This acquirement of a knowledge of the divine will is not the work of an instant; it results from patient and persistent spiritual study, prayer, and meditation. Even Jesus, with His exalted understanding, found it necessary to pray all night. All who have found the peace and the power of God have testified to the necessity of using prayer in the soul's victory.

One should not intellectually will to bring about results for oneself or for another. The difference between the personal will and the universal will can be known by one who practices thought control in the silence.

Affirmations made in the head alone are followed by a feeling of tension, as if bands were drawn across the forehead. When this state of mind sinks back into the subconsciousness, the nerves become tense; if the practice is continued, nervous prostration follows.

Stubborn, willful, resistant states of mind congest the life flow; they are followed by cramps and congestion. The will often compels the use of the various organs of the body beyond their normal capacity, and the results are found in strained nerves and strained muscles and in impaired sight and impaired hearing. Disobedient children have earache, showing the direct result that self-will has on the nerves of the ear. Deaf persons should be treated for freedom from willfulness and obstinacy. In the present state of race consciousness, all people use the intellectual will to excess. The remedy is daily relaxation, meditation, prayer.

Will, as exercised by man, is the negative pole of the great executive force of the universe. The recognition of this in silent meditation opens the will to the inflow of this mighty, moving principle, and the power that moves to action the members of the body reaches into the invisible realm of ideas and controls the elements. It was comprehension of the will universal that enabled Jesus to say to the wind and the waves, "Peace, be still."

Life, liberty, and the pursuit of happiness are the inalienable rights of man, and they should never be interfered with. Hypnotism, mesmerism, and mediumship are based on the submission of one will to another. The one who desires control demands another's submission in mind and body to his own willed thoughts and words of directive power. The effect on the one who submits is always weakening and, if continued, results in a mental negation that makes him the victim of evil influences too numerous to mention.

"Not my will, but thine, be done" is one of the most far-reaching affirmations of Jesus, and those who follow Him and keep His sayings are finding great peace and relaxation of mind and body.

Jesus, the mighty helper, is always present with those who are earnestly seeking to be Christians and to keep the divine law.

CHAPTER 10

❦

Spiritual Law and Order

THE TWENTY-THIRD chapter of Matthew is a philippic against ritualism. Jesus arraigns the scribes and the Pharisees before the bar of the divine law and charges them with a long list of crimes committed in the name of religion. He makes charge after charge of delinquency in spiritual observance of the law and warns His disciples and the multitudes to beware of the works of these blind leaders of the blind. Among other accusations, He says:

"Yea, they bind heavy burdens and grievous to be borne, and lay them on men's shoulders . . . all their works they do to be seen of men . . . they . . . love the chief place at feasts, and the chief seats in the synagogues . . . and to be called of men, Rabbi. But be not ye called Rabbi: for one is your teacher, and all ye are brethren. And call no man your father on the earth: for one is your Father, *even* he who is in heaven. Neither be ye called masters: for one is your master, *even* the Christ. But he that is greatest among you shall be your servant. And whosoever shall exalt himself shall be humbled; and whosoever shall humble himself shall be exalted.

But woe unto you, scribes and Pharisees, hypocrites! because ye shut the kingdom of heaven against men: for ye enter not in yourselves, neither suffer ye them that are entering in to enter.

Woe unto you, scribes and Pharisees, hypocrites! for ye

compass sea and land to make one proselyte; and when he is become so, ye make him twofold more a son of hell than yourselves. . . .

Woe unto you, scribes and Pharisees, hypocrites! for ye tithe mint and anise and cummin, and have left undone the weightier matters of the law, justice, and mercy, and faith: but these ye ought to have done, and not to have left the other undone. Ye blind guides, that strain out the gnat, and swallow the camel!

Woe unto you, scribes and Pharisees, hypocrites! for ye cleanse the outside of the cup and of the platter, but within they are full from extortion and excess. Thou blind Pharisee, cleanse first the inside of the cup and of the platter, that the outside thereof may become clean also. . . .

Woe unto you, scribes and Pharisees, hypocrites! for ye build the sepulchres of the prophets, and garnish the tombs of the righteous, and say, If we had been in the days of our fathers, we should not have been partakers with them in the blood of the prophets."

All these "woes" are to those who are living in the letter instead of in the spirit of the law. But Jesus did not condemn religion, nor religious organizations. His denunciations were aimed at those who profess to teach and to follow the law but fall short in carrying it out in their lives.

Right here, however, religious teachers should be on their guard in framing tenets for religious organizations. Do not dogmatize in creed, or statement of Being, as a governing rule of thought and action for those who join your organization. These things are limitations, and they often prevent free development because of foolish insistence on consistency. The creed that you write today may not fit the viewpoint of tomorrow; hence the safe and sure religious foundation for all men is that laid down by Jesus: "The Spirit of truth . . . shall guide you into all the truth." A statement setting forth the teaching of a religious institution is essential, but compelling clauses should be omitted.

The Mosaic law had been framed for the benefit of the Hebrews, but their priesthood made it a hindrance to spiritual progress. Jesus was an iconoclast, and He made it His special business to break nearly every rule of action that the priests had evolved. For example, they had thirty-nine prohibitions in regard to the observance of the Sabbath. These were nearly all trivial, such as preparing food, riding on a beast, drawing water, carrying a burden, going on a journey; yet death was the penalty for transgression. Labor of any kind on the Sabbath was punishable by death. To roll grains of wheat in the hand was considered labor, so when the apostles of Jesus plucked the ears of grain the Pharisees said to Him: "Behold, why do they on the sabbath day that which is not lawful?" Then Jesus gave them a sermon on freedom from their narrow rules governing the Sabbath day; He ended with, "The Sabbath was made for man, and not man for the sabbath."

The fact is that the Sabbath as an institution was established by man. God does not rest from His works every seventh day, and there is no evidence that there has ever been a moment's cessation in the activity of the universe. Those who stickle most for Sabbath-day observance are met on every hand by the evidence of perpetual activity on the part of Him whom they claim to champion.

We are told that trees, flowers, planets, suns, stars, and sidereal systems are the work of God; that it is God who sustains and governs, controls and directs them. Yet trees, flowers, planets, suns, and stars are active the first day and the seventh day of the week, just the same as on other days.

It would seem proper that, if God ordained a certain day of rest and rested on that day Himself, as is claimed, He should give some evidence of it in His creations; but He has not done this, so far as anybody knows. The Truth is that Divine Mind rests in a perpetual Sabbath, and that which seems work is not work at all. When man becomes so at-one with the Father-Mind as to feel it consciously, he also recognizes this eternal peace, in which all things are accomplished. He then knows that he is not subject to any condition whatsoever and that he is "lord even of the sabbath."

Man can never exercise dominion until he knows who and what he is and, knowing, brings forth that knowledge into the external by exercising it in divine order, which is mind, idea, and manifestation. Jesus horrified the Jews by healing the sick, plucking grain, and performing other acts, which to them were sacrilegious, on the Sabbath day. The Jews manufactured these sacred days and observances, just as our Puritan fathers made life a burden by their rigid and absurd laws governing the religious acts of the people. For centuries the Jews had been binding themselves to the wheel of religious bigotry, and the Puritans accomplished a like task in a shorter time. The length of time was the only difference.

But Jesus knew all the exacting ecclesiastical rules to be man-made. "He himself knew what was in man," and He attempted to disabuse those benighted minds of their error. He tried to make them understand that the Sabbath was made for man, not man for the Sabbath. They had wound themselves up in religious ceremonies until their ecclesiastical machinery dominated every act of their lives. Not only were they subjects of their sacred law, but they were its absolute slaves.

It was the mission of Jesus to break down this mental structure which had been reared through ages of blind servitude to form and ritual. The Mosaic law had been made so rigid that it held the Jews in its icy bonds to the exclusion of all reason and common sense. Jesus saw this, and He purposely overstepped the bounds of religious propriety in order that He might more effectively impress on them the fact that the old Mosaic dispensation was at an end. He told them that He did not come to break the law, but to fulfill it. He was speaking of the true law of God, and not their external rules of sacrifice, penance, Sabbath observance, and the like. He knew that these rules were of the letter—purely perfunctory; that they were in reality hindrances to the expression of the inner spiritual life.

Man cannot grow into the understanding of

Spirit, nor be obedient to its leading, if he is hampered by external rules of action. No man-made law is strong enough, or true enough, or exact enough, to be a permanent guide for anyone.

If in your path toward the light you have fixed a point of achievement that attainment of which you think will satisfy you, you have made a limitation that you must eventually destroy. There is no stopping place for God; there is no stopping place for man.

If the church goes back to Moses and the old dispensation, ignoring the lessons of Jesus, it is no guide for you. If you want to be His disciple, you must unite your spirit with His.

Paul, with his dominant beliefs in the efficiency of the old way, at times loaded those beliefs upon the free doctrine of Jesus, but that is no reason why *you* should be burdened with them. You can never be what the Father wants you to be until you recognize that you stand alone, with Him as your sole and original guide, just as much alone as if you were the first and only man. You can hear His Word when you have erased from your mind all tradition and authority of men, and His Word will never sound clearly in your mind until you have done this.

It is not necessary that you despise the scriptures of the Jews, of the Hindus, or of any people, but you are to take them for what they are—the records of men as to what their experiences have been in communing with the omnipresent God. As Jesus said to the Pharisees: "Ye preach the scriptures, because ye think that in them ye have eternal life; and these are they which bear witness of me; and ye will not come to me, that ye may have life." From all sacred writings you can get many wonderfully helpful hints as to the work of God in the minds of men. You should treasure all pure words of Truth that have been written by brothers in the Spirit, yet they are not authority for you nor should you be moved to do anything simply because it is written in the Scriptures as a law of God for the specific guidance of man.

Mortal man loves to be dominated and whipped into line by rituals and masters, but divine man, the man of God, oversteps all such childish circumscribings and goes direct to the Father for all instruction.

It is your privilege to be as free as the birds, the trees, the flowers. "They toil not, neither do they spin," but are always obedient to the divine instinct, and their every day is a Sabbath. They stand in no fear of an angry God, though they build a nest, spread a leaf, or open a petal on the first day or on the seventh day. All days are holy days to them. They live in the holy Omnipresence, always doing the will of Him who sent them. It is our duty to do likewise. That which is instinct in them is conscious, loving obedience in us. When we have resolved to be attentive to the voice of the Father and to do His will at any cost, we are freed from the bondage of all man-made laws. Our bonds—in the form of some fear of transgressing the divine law—slip away into the sea of nothingness, and we sit on the shore and praise the loving All-Good that we are never more to be frightened by an accusing conscience or by the possibility of misunderstanding His law.

But we are not to quarrel with our brother over observance of the Sabbath. If he insists that the Lord should be worshiped on the seventh day, we shall joyfully join him on that day; and if he holds that the first day is the holy day, we again acquiesce. Not only do we do God's service in praise, song, and thanksgiving on the seventh day and the first day, but also on every day. Our minds are open to God every moment. We are ever ready to acknowledge His holy presence in our hearts; it is a perpetual Sunday with us. We are not satisfied with one day out of the seven set aside for religious observance, but, like the birds, the trees, and the flowers, we join in a glad refrain of thanksgiving in and out of season. When we work and when we sleep we are ever praising the holy Omnipresence that burns its lamp of love perpetually in our hearts and keeps forever the light of life before us.

This is the observance of God's holy day that the divinely wise forever recognize. It is not in churches nor in temples reared by man in any form that he finds communion with the Father. He has found the true church, the heaven within himself. There he meets the Father face to face; he does not greet Him as one removed to a distant place, to whom he communicates his wishes through some prophet or priest, but each for himself goes to the Father in closest fellowship.

"God so loved the world, that he gave his only begotten Son, that whosoever believeth on him should not perish, but have eternal life." This does not mean that a personal man, named Jesus of Nazareth, was sent forth as a special propitiation for the sins of the world, or that the only available route into the Father's presence lies through such a person. It simply means that God has provided a way by which all men may come consciously into His presence in their own souls. That way is through the only begotten Son of God, the Christ consciousness, which Jesus demonstrated. This consciousness is the always present Son of the Father, dwelling as a spiritual seed in each of us and ready to germinate and grow at our will. The Son of God is in essence the life, the love, and the wisdom of the Father himself; through us the Son is made manifest as a living individuality. He cannot be killed out entirely; He ever grows at the center of our being as the "*light* which lighteth every man, coming into the world."

To believe on the Son is to come to His terms of expression. It is the simplest thing in the world. Just believe that He is the only begotten Son of the Father. Do not believe that there are other sons wiser than He is, and that from them you can get wisdom, guidance, and understanding, but know that He is indeed the only begotten Son.

This distinction is a vital point for you to apprehend, and when you have once apprehended it your journey back to the Father's house is easy. "No one cometh unto the Father, but by me," the only Son is constantly saying in your heart, and you must not ignore His presence if you would know the sweets of the heavenly home where the love of God forever burns its incense of peace, plenty, and contentment. Let Christ be formed in you, was Paul's admonition. This is not hyperbole or an abstraction, but a statement of a definite rule of procedure, which you can discover and prove by making terms with this indwelling Son of the Father. His terms are not severe. They are simply obedience, obedience.

Jesus of Nazareth found this inner flame and let it burn all through His body. It so lighted Him up that His presence warms all sin-sick men to this very day.

But no one lives by reflection. You could not live a moment if it were not for this only begotten Son of the Father within you. So you cannot live and grow on the reflected light of Jesus of Nazareth. The only begotten Son of God must come forth in you as it did in Jesus. Then your life will be permanent, and the discords of the flesh will drop away forever; then will your Sabbath be revealed to you.

The redemptive, restorative, and regenerative work that the Christ of God did through Jesus is not ignored by Christian metaphysicians. However, the salvation of men from the sins of mortality was not accomplished by the man Jesus alone; it was through the power of the Christ in Jesus that God provided purified life and substance for the corruptible bodies of men. Jesus' body was used as the vehicle through which a fresh and pure life stream and a regenerative substance were made available to all those who will accept them. The redeemed substance of the body of the Lord is just as essential to full salvation as His blood. Also, this is a salvation that is to be attained here on earth, and not after death. Jesus' body was metamorphosed or changed from the corruptible flesh of the average man to the incorruptible substance of divine man. When we eat and drink of His body we shall become like Him in body perfection. This process of restoration of the body of man to its original purity is the basis of divine or spiritual healing. The complete redemption of the body may not be accomplished in one incarnation, but whoever accepts the Christ as life and substance, and conforms to righteous living as taught by the Spirit of Truth, will finally sit with Jesus on the throne of dominion over disease and death.

There is a law of spiritual and mental growth constantly at work in the mind, a law that is raising man from sense consciousness, or Egypt, to spiritual consciousness, or Canaan. *Moses* means "drawn out," and represents in Scripture symbology this progressive or drawing-out process, which works from within out. As applied to the universe, this upward trend of all things is called by material science "the evolutionary law." In our spiritual interpretation we observe the working of the law in the individual, because by that method we can bring home the lesson. Through intelligent use of the hints given, we apply the lesson to ourselves with great profit.

Involution always precedes evolution. That which is involved in mind evolves through matter. Joseph down in Egypt portrays the involution in matter of a high spiritual idea. The spiritual idea attracted other ideas like it (Joseph's relatives), and they greatly multiplied in the land of Egypt. It is estimated that the Children of Israel increased from a few score to at least two million. This illustrates the fact that spiritual thoughts grow with tremendous rapidity in consciousness when they have Truth as a nucleus.

Yet these true thoughts that have so greatly multiplied are in slavery to the Egyptians (sense nature), and a special effort has to be made to free them. We have our high ideals, but because the temporal life seems so important, those ideals are made to work in the most menial ways to carry on this passing show. A time comes, however, when we rebel at this tyranny; we rise up in so-called righteous indignation, and in violent ways we kill out the opposing sense nature, as Moses killed the Egyptian. But this is not the right way. We are not to be liberated by suppression of sense, or by violent overcoming, but by a steady step-by-step demonstration over every error. The Lord recognizes the rights of the physical man, and He hardens Pharaoh's heart that he may sustain for a season his rightful place in consciousness.

The fleeing of Moses to the wilderness represents

the discipline that we must undergo when we seek the exalted One. *Horeb* means "solitude"; that is, we have to go into the solitude of the within and lead our flock of thoughts to the back of the wilderness, where dwells the exalted One, the I AM, whose kingdom is good judgment. There we are in training forty years, or until we arrive at a four-sided or balanced state of mind. Then the light of intuition or flame of fire burns in our hearts, yet it is not consumed—there is no loss of substance. In brain thinking there is a vibratory process that uses up nerve tissue, but in the wisdom that comes from the heart, the "bush" or tissue is not consumed. This thinking in wisdom is "holy ground," or substance in its spiritual wholeness; that is, the idea of substance in Divine Mind. When this holy ground is approached by man he must take off from his understanding all limited thoughts of the Absolute— he must put his shoes off his feet.

It is at this wisdom center within us that God proclaims Himself to be the Father of fathers, the God of Abraham, Isaac, and Jacob; thus our real Father is revealed to us as Spirit.

In our communion in the silence with the light within us, the bondage of the higher to the lower is made clear to us, and the true way of release is indicated. We see the possibilities of man and the goodness of the "promised land," to which we can raise every thought. But Moses was very meek—we feel our inability, and we say, "Who am I that I should go unto Pharaoh, and that I should bring forth the children of Israel out of Egypt?" Then we have the assurance that God's power is with us— "Certainly I will be with thee." It is in the recognition of the power and the presence of God that all our strength and all our ability lie. Jesus, the great spiritual master, said, "The Father abiding in me doeth his works."

All great structures are erected on firm foundations. Anyone whom the Lord calls to a work will succeed in the end, if he lays his foundation deep and strong in spiritual understanding. This understanding is attained through meditation and study in the silence. Moses was forty years separated from the busy haunts of men, learning to know God "face to face."

In our silent meditations and prayers we must infuse into the inner mind realms the same energy that, used without, would make us notable in some worldly achievement. But unless we do this inner work and lay the foundation of strength and power in the subjective mind, we shall find ourselves in failing health when called upon for extra exertion in some great effort.

The angel of the Lord, the flame of fire, and the bush are all within the consciousness of man, becoming manifest through interior concentration. The bush is a nerve center through which the universal life energy runs like electricity over a wire, making a light but not consuming. The angel is the presiding intelligence that is always present in every life action or function.

Man is first attracted by the phenomenal side of spiritual things; then, when he gives his attention for the purpose of knowing the cause, the Lord reveals Himself. When Moses turned aside and began to investigate, he found that he was on holy ground. The forces of Spirit at the center of man's body are so intense that the outer consciousness cannot stand the current and hold itself together; absolutely pure in essence, this inner fire must be approached by the pure spiritual thought. Removing the sandals is symbolical of taking all material concepts from the understanding.

The Spirit of the Lord has been evolving in the subconsciousness, incarnation after incarnation. This I AM was the moving factor in Abraham, Isaac, and Jacob—the Lord is present in all.

Egypt is strictly material consciousness. It pertains to the physical sense of life, the corporeal organism. Canaan is life and substance in a radiant state; here Spirit finds its natural expression. The thoughts that belong in the radiant body have become slaves of material sense, and the higher Self, the Lord, would set them free. But to do this the higher understanding must become part of their consciousness. All things are created by and through certain states of mind or consciousness.

The higher spiritual consciousness is infused into the mortal or personal consciousness. Personal *I* must take on supreme I AM. When this is first experienced there is a feeling of inefficiency. But the Lord's promise to be present under all circumstances is a mighty inner assurance of spiritual law and order.

Christian metaphysicians have learned by experience the power of words and thoughts sent forth in the name of the supreme I AM. The word of the Lord spoken by naturally weak men has produced marvelous results, because they set their minds not on their own weak ideas of man and his abilities, but upon the mightiness of the great I AM. The Lord God, speaking through them, does the work of the Master. "I speak not from myself: but the Father abiding in me [supreme I AM] doeth his works."

Moses and Pharaoh represent two forces at work in the consciousness—especially that part of it pertaining to the body. Moses represents the evolutionary force of new ideas that have grown in the subconsciousness; these forces struggle with the old states of limitation and material ignorance, trying to rise out of their depths into a higher life expression. The rising into a higher life is symbolized by the man Moses, whose name means "drawn out." As a child he was drawn out of the water, a negative yet universal condition of life evolution. Pharaoh represents the force that rules the body under the material régime. The Lord is the universal law, whose impulse is always upward and onward. It is found by those who are undergoing the regenerative process that the Scriptures symbolically describe in the story of Moses, that these two forces are constantly at work in consciousness, one holding to old ideas and striving to perpetuate them in form and the other idealizing the new and bending every effort to break away from material bondage and rise above its limitations. Paul says, "The flesh lusteth against the Spirit, and the Spirit against the flesh." Looking at it from the personal standpoint, we are likely to cry out in this struggle, "Who shall deliver me out of the body of this death?" But as philosophers, with an understanding of the law of change, we balance ourselves between these two forces and let them work out under the equilibrium of the universal preserver of all forms, the Lord.

Here is consolation for those who chafe under the whips and cords of the regenerative law. Because of their many defeats and the snail's pace at which they progress, they think that they are off the track. However, they are not. They will attain their good if they persevere and patiently wait upon the Lord. If the energy of Spirit were instantly poured into the body, it would destroy the organism because of the impurities of the flesh, but by and through the evolutionary adjustment of the natural man, the Spirit not only preserves but raises up the substance and life of the organism. The purpose of our spiritual thoughts (the Children of Israel) down in the body (Egypt) is to raise up the body—gradually to infuse into it a more enduring life and substance. At the same time our spiritual thoughts get the substance (corn) that is to sustain their existence in the world of phenomena.

When you affirm the spirituality of the body and yearn for release from its bondage, you are making

demands on Pharaoh. In fear that he will all at once
lose his hold on life, he hardens his heart, and
sometimes the Lord, the universal law of equilibrium, hardens it *for* him. Then there seems a failure
to attain that which you have tried to demonstrate.
But a step has been taken in the evolution of the
body, and you will find that you are gradually becoming stronger, both physically and spiritually.

There are climaxes in this refining trend of the
consciousness, and in these we make a signal effort
and realize a great uplift. "Jewels of silver, and jewels of gold" represent wisdom and love in an external sense, which are to be asked or demanded by the
Children of Israel. (The word *borrow* in the King
James Version is an error.) The meaning is that we
are to affirm that all wisdom and all love, even in
their most external manifestations, are spiritual. By
so affirming we put Spirit into control both within
and without ourselves and do away with the external ruling power, which is the "firstborn in the
land of Egypt." The firstborn of every state of consciousness is the personal *I*. When the flood of light
from the universal is let in through our declaration
of the one wisdom and one love, this *I* of every
mortal state of consciousness is slain, and there is a
"great cry throughout all the land of Egypt."

We may mentally have made our truest statements and seemingly complied with all the law,
yet Pharaoh does not let our people go—there is no
realization of freedom in the body consciousness.
Another step toward freedom is necessary, which is

typified in the Feast of the Passover.

In every change of consciousness on the physical plane, there is a breaking down of some cells and a building up of other cells to take their place. Mentally this is denial and affirmation, and this process in the body is the result of these two movements in the mind which have occurred at some previous period. We let go of the animal life and take hold of the spiritual by giving up consciously to this "passing over" process, which takes place when the old cells are replaced by the new. The lamb that is killed and eaten in the night represents giving up the animal life in the obscurity of the mortal body. The command is that the lamb shall be without spot or blemish and be wholly eaten after being roasted with fire. This refers to the complete transmutation and surrender of the human life after it has been purified by the fires of regeneration. Fire represents the positive, affirmative state of mind, as opposed to the negative or watery state. The Children of Israel were commanded not to let the lamb be "sodden." *Sodden* is an Old English past participle of *seethe*. We are not to allow the life in our organism to simmer and stew with the worries and negative words of mortality, but we must set it afire with strong words of absolute Truth.

This is to show us that there must be a physical as well as a mental sacrifice and that "the whole congregation of the children of Israel" will join in it; that is, the whole consciousness of spiritual desire will acquiesce. Many metaphysicians think that it is not necessary to change the habits of the sense man—that one has only to keep one's thoughts right and the flesh will thereby be wholly regulated. But the Scripture teaches that there must be a conscious physical change before the complete demonstration in mind and body is manifest. Thoughts work themselves out in things, and we get the full result of their work only when we follow them consciously every step of the way and help them along. Watch your thoughts as they work their way through your organism, and, if you find that some pure thought of spiritual life is striving to free the life in the appetites and passions of your physical Egypt, help it by consciously elevating that life to the open door of your mind. This is typified by putting the blood of the lamb on the two side posts and on the lintel of the door of the house. Do not be afraid to express your inner life to the Lord, for only in perfect candor and childlike innocence can man come under the protection of the divine law.

So long as there is a hidden, secret use of God's life in our habits and ways that we are not willing that all should know, just so long will the bondage of Egypt's Pharaoh hold us in its clutches. The whole man must be pure, and his inner life must be made so open and free that he will not be afraid to blazon it upon the very doors of his house where all who pass may read. Then the Lord will execute His judgment, and those who have purified the life of the lamb of the body will escape the messenger, or thought, of death.

‒‒‒‒‒

CHAPTER 11

Zeal—Enthusiasm

THE EGO, the free *I*, the imperishable and unchangeable essence of Spirit, which man is, chooses every state of consciousness and every condition in which it functions. It does not create the basic substances that enter into these mental structures, for these substances have been provided from the beginning, but it gives form and character to them in consciousness, as men build houses of lumber, stone, or whatever material they may choose in the manifest.

These mental states are all constructed under the dynamic power of the great universal impulse that lies back of all action—enthusiasm, or zeal. Zeal is the mighty force that incites the winds, the tides, the storms; it urges the planet on its course, and spurs the ant to great exertion. To be without zeal is to be without the zest of living. Zeal and enthusiasm incite to glorious achievement in every aim and ideal that the mind conceives. Zeal is the impulse to go forward, the urge behind all things. Without zeal, stagnation, inertia, death would prevail throughout the universe. The man without zeal is like an engine without steam or an electric motor without a current. Energy is zeal in motion, and energy is the forerunner of every effect.

If you desire a thing, you set in motion the machinery of the universe to gain possession of it, but you must be zealous in the pursuit in order to attain the object of your desire. Desire goes before every act of your life, hence it is good. It is the very essence of good; it is God Himself in a phase of life. When they called Jesus good, He said: "Why callest thou me good? none is good save one, *even* God." So the universal desire for achievement, giving its mighty impulse to all things, is divinely good. Divine enthusiasm is no respecter of persons or things. It makes no distinctions. It moves to new forms of expression even that which appears corrupt. It tints the cheek of the innocent babe, gleams from the eye of the treacherous savage, and lights in purity the face of the saint.

Some have named this universal life-impulse "God," and have left the impression that it is all of God and that all the attributes of God-Mind are therefore involved as a conscious entity in every situation where life is manifest. In this they lack discrimination. God's Spirit goes forth in mighty streams of life, love, substance, and intelligence. Each of these attributes is conscious only of the principle involved in it and in the work that it has to do. Though it is man's mission to combine these inexhaustible potentialities under divine law, man is free to do as he wills. But the divine law cannot be broken, and it holds man responsible for the result of his labors. Man cannot corrupt the inherent purity of any of God's attributes, but he can unwisely combine them in states of consciousness that bring dissatisfaction and incompleteness to him. It is his privilege to learn the harmonious relations of all the chords of life and to arrange them on the staff of existence with such masterly art that no discord can be detected. Then life becomes to him a song of joy, and he absolutely knows that in its ultimate all is good.

Never repress the impulse, the force, the zeal welling up within you. Commune with it in spirit and praise it for its great energy and efficiency in action. At the same time analyze and direct its course. As zeal alone, it is without intelligence or discretion as to results. As Jesus taught His disciples and combined their various talents, so every man must grow in wisdom and zeal. You are not to repress but to guide the spirit of enthusiasm, which in co-operation with wisdom, will bring you happiness and satisfaction.

Zeal is the affirmative impulse of existence; its command is "Go forward!" Through this impulse man forms many states of consciousness that he ultimately tires of. They may have served a good purpose in their day in the grand scheme of creation, but as man catches sight of higher things, zeal urges him forward to their attainment.

Let your zeal be tempered with wisdom. "The zeal of thy house hath eaten me up" means that the zeal faculty has become so active intellectually that it has consumed the vitality and left nothing for spiritual growth. One may even become so zealous for the spread of Truth as to bring on nervous prostration.

"Take time to be holy." Turn a portion of your zeal to do God's will to the establishing of His kingdom within you. Do not put all your enthusiasm into teaching, preaching, healing, and helping others; help yourself. Many enthusiastic spiritual workers have let their zeal to demonstrate Truth to others rob them of the power to demonstrate Truth for themselves. Do not let your zeal run away with your judgment. Some persons get so fired with zeal when they first tackle a job that they quickly grow tired, and eventually get "fired" from every job that they tackle.

Watch the first pull of a giant locomotive; note how it slowly but steadily moves forward, almost by inches at first but gradually increasing, until its mile-long train swiftly disappears in the distance.

Man is a dynamo of pent-up power, but he needs judgment in its use. Even love (John), the "greatest thing in the world," is linked in the twelve-power integration of Jesus with James (judgment). Jesus called these two brothers "Sons of thunder," comparing the effect of their combined power to the tremendous vibrations set up by unrestrained electrical energy. Judgment says to Love, "Look before you leap." Do not let unselfish zeal and enthusiasm for the loved one run away with your judgment. Remember that these two are brothers and that you should sit on the throne of your I AM dominion, with love on the right hand and judgment on the left, judging the twelve tribes of Israel. In these symbols we see portrayed the poise and mastery of regenerated man, directing and disciplining all his thought-people in wisdom and in love.

Even doctors are beginning to take notice of the emotional contests that take place between love and wisdom in our nervous system. Some of them say that indigestion may be caused by the disturbance that our emotions cause in the delicate nerve aggregations at the solar plexus, and that permanent stomach troubles may result. Metaphysicians have always taught that the contending vibrations or "thunder" between love and wisdom cause not only acute but chronic diseases of stomach and heart.

Heart says, "I love," and Wisdom says, "But you can't have what you love"; contention follows, and night and day the nerves are pounded by the warring emotions.

Love disappointed may lower the vitality to the vanishing point, while some physical disease is blamed.

Innumerable combinations of thoughts and their attendant emotions are constantly sending their vibrations or "thundering" to various parts of the body through the nerve cables that lead out from the many ganglionic centers.

Jesus had two apostles named Simon, but they represent different talents or faculties of man's mind. Simon Peter represents receptivity from above, and Simon the Cananaean represents receptivity from below. *Simon* means "hearing" and *Canaan* means "zeal." The Canaanites dwelt in the lowlands, so we know that the faculty designated by Simon the

Cananaean has its origin in the body consciousness.

But the receptivity to, and the zeal for, the Truth that were manifested by Simon the Cananaean were lifting him to spiritual consciousness. This is symbolized in Acts 1:13, where it is written, "And when they were come in, they went up into the upper chamber, where they were abiding." Among them is mentioned "Simon the Zealot."

To grow spiritually we should always be careful to exercise our zeal in spiritual ways, since Christians are apt to fall into commercial ways in carrying forward the Lord's work. We should remember that Jesus said, "God is spirit: and they that worship him must worship in spirit and truth." When Jesus cast the money-changers out of the Temple, His disciples remembered that it was written, "Zeal for thy house shall eat me up." In this act Jesus was casting the commercial bargaining thoughts out of His body temple. This is explained in the context, John 2:18. The Jews said: "What sign showest thou unto us, seeing that thou doest these things? Jesus answered and said unto them, Destroy this temple, and in three days I will raise it up. . . . But he spake of the temple of his body."

Whatever takes place in the world about us has its counterpart in some thought process in our body. Every invention of man is a duplication of some activity in the human body. The explosion of gasoline in an automobile cylinder is copied from the explosion of nerve substance in the cell centers of the body. The nerve fluid is conducted to a nerve chamber, corresponding to an automobile combustion chamber, where it is electrified and the energy liberated. In the human body spiritual zeal, that is, enthusiasm, electrifies the nerve substance, which breaks forth into energy.

Thoughts build nerve and brain centers that serve as distributors of the vital substance manufactured in the body. The vitamins in the food that we eat are stored up by the body chemistry and liberated in thought and action.

Every thought and emanation of mind liberates some of this stored substance. We, the controlling intelligence, with our conscious mind direct these processes in a manner quite similar to that employed by the driver of an automobile. An automobile driver should be familiar with the mechanism of his car. But in the great majority of cases the driver knows merely enough to perform a few mechanical motions, and the car does the rest.

So the mass of humans know but little about the delicate mind-and-body interaction. They perform a few necessary superficial acts, call in the doctor when anything goes wrong, and in the end dump the old "boat" at the junk pile.

Extraordinary zeal in the accomplishment of some ideal develops what is called genius. Jesus of Nazareth was undoubtedly the greatest genius that this earth has ever developed. He is not usually named among the geniuses of the earth, because He was a genius of such transcendental character that He is classed with the gods. He did manifest the mind of

God as no other has ever done, yet He was a man, and herein lies His genius:

In His humanity He developed extraordinary ability in spiritual wisdom, love, and power. There have been men who have told us about God, but none who have demonstrated the wisdom and power of God as Jesus did. His zeal in doing the will of God made Him a spiritual genius in human form.

Like others who manifest original genius, Jesus got His genius from within. He was not known to have been taught in the theological schools of His day, yet He exhibited a mental acumen and understanding of religion that astonished His associates. They exclaimed in effect, "Where did this man get wisdom, never having studied."

Genius is the accumulated zeal of the individual in some chosen field of life action. The idea that God has arbitrarily endowed some persons with abilities superior to others is not good logic, and makes God a partisan. God has no favorites, notwithstanding the fact that the Scriptures sometimes so interpret Him. "God is no respecter of persons." "This is my beloved Son, in whom I am well pleased," is the ideal or spiritual man, the Messiah, the Christ man, who is the pattern given to every man to follow.

However, we see on every hand evidences of pronounced diversity in human character, and, looking at life superficially, we think that God has given advantages in mind, body, and affairs to some men that He has not given to others.

But what we see with the eye of flesh is only the physical manifestation of man. Spirit and mind must be taken into consideration and become factors in our reasoning before we can know a man and properly estimate the whole man.

The body represents but one third of man's being. Man is Spirit, soul, and body. The Spirit is that in man which says I AM, and has existed from eternity. Spirit is potential man—soul is demonstrated man. Soul is man's memory, conscious and subconscious. We have carried along in our subconscious mind the memory of every experience that we have had since we began to think and act for ourselves. The soul is the mind, and the mind is the man.

The race to which we belong on this planet began thinking and acting in self-consciousness many millions of years ago. God alone knows the exact age of every man. Jesus said, "The very hairs of your head are all numbered."

Every experience, every achievement, every failure, and every success is remembered and stored up in the subconscious mind. A new soul is not created with every physical birth. A physical birth simply means that a soul is taking on another body. Every man inhabiting this earth and the psychic realms immediately surrounding it has gone through this process of dying and being reincarnated many times. You who read these lines have had experience as a thinking, free-acting soul for millions of years, instead of the score or three score that mortal man usually counts. Emerson said, "Be not deceived by dimples and curls; that child is a thousand years old."

Then the question arises, "Do we always get the fruit of our earthly acts in some future earthly life?" Certainly, "Whatsoever a man soweth, that shall he also reap." Here in this earth is the place of harvest. When a man relinquishes his hold on brain and nervous system, he gives up the only avenue through which he can adequately express himself.

So death is the great enemy to be overcome, as taught in Scripture. Death came into the world through Adamic ignorance, and it must go out through Christ understanding.

Genius is the breaking forth of the accumulated achievements of a man in that field of activity for which he has been very zealous in many incarnations. Mozart at the age of four played the organ without instruction. Where did he get such marvelous musical ability? A history of his soul would show that he had cultivated music for ages, carrying from one incarnation to another his zeal for the harmony of sound, until he became the very soul of music.

The genius of Shakespeare was the accumulated experience of a man who had been poet and philosopher since the "morning stars sang together."

Let no man think that he can retire from living. Do not shirk the responsibilities of life. You have made them and you can unmake them. A way of escape has been provided for every one of us. That way is to overcome mistakes by incorporating into mind and heart the attributes of the Christ Mind.

"Travail until Christ be formed in you."

Let us think of man as a king having twelve sons or princes, who execute his will. Each of these princes has a throne, or brain and nerve center, from which he issues his orders and distributes his goods.

Jesus illustrated this in Matthew 19:28: "Verily I say unto you, that ye who have followed me, in the regeneration when the Son of man shall sit on the throne of his glory, ye also shall sit upon twelve thrones, judging the twelve tribes of Israel."

Simon the Zealot has his center or throne of dominion in the body at the base of the brain, named by physiology the *medulla oblongata*. Simon the Zealot from his throne at the medulla imparts especial energy to the ears, eyes, nose, mouth, and sensory nervous system. When man enters into the understanding of his dominion, power, and directive ability in Christ, he educates his disciples, or sons, and shows them how to execute the law established in divine principle for man.

We all are kings in Christ. But with Him we must realize that "my kingdom is not of this world." Our dominion is over our own thoughts, emotions, and passions. Our disciples will do what we tell them and continue to do it after they have been sufficiently instructed and assisted in the use of the Word. Remember that mind rules in both the within and the without, the visible and the invisible, the high and the low.

To help Simon the Zealot do his work, center

your attention for a moment at the base of your brain and quietly affirm that infinite energy and intelligence are pouring forth in zeal—enthusiasm. Then follow in imagination a set of motor nerves that lead out from the medulla to the eyes, affirming all the time the presence and power of energy and intelligence now manifesting in your eyes.

For the ears affirm energy and intelligence, adding, *"Be you open."* For the nose affirm energy and intelligence, adding, *"The purity of Spirit infolds you."* For the mouth carry the life current to the root of the tongue, with the thought of *freedom.*

At the root of the tongue is situated the throne of another disciple, Philip. When you carry the zeal current from its medulla center and connect it with the throne of Philip, a mighty vibration is set up that affects the whole sympathetic nervous system. In this treatment you will strengthen your voice, revitalize your teeth, and indirectly impart energy to your digestion.

It was at Cana of Galilee, the nerve center in the throat, that Jesus turned water into wine. Metaphysically this miracle is accomplished when we in Spirit realize that the union (wedding) of the fluid life of the body with the spiritual life at this power center makes a new element, symbolized by wine. When the chemistry of the body and the dynamics of the mind are united, a third element is brought forth, and man feels that, "in Christ, *he is* a new creature."

~~~~~~~

CHAPTER 12

Renunciation

ALL CHRISTIANS who have had experiences variously described as "change of heart," "salvation," "conversion," and "sanctification" will admit that, before they experienced the great change of consciousness represented by these names, they had been "convicted of sin" or had determined to give up the ways of the world and do the will of God. The sinners most open to reform are those who sin in the flesh. The hardest to reach are the self-satisfied moralists or religionists. Jesus said to such, "Verily I say unto you, that the publicans and the harlots go into the kingdom of God before you." One who is living up to man-made morals or religious standards is not repentant, and he makes no room in his mind for new and higher ideals of life and Truth. Unless our repentance is accompanied by sacrifice, we are still in our sins. "Apart from shedding of blood there is no remission." The blood represents the life, and when the life of the flesh is given up, the beasts of the body are literally killed and their blood, or life, carries away the dead cells. This was symbolically illustrated by Jesus when He sent the demons, or evils, into the swine (Mt. 8:32).

A change of mind effects a corresponding change

in the body. If the thoughts are lifted up, the whole organism is raised to higher rates of vibration. If the system has been burdened with congestion of any kind, a higher life energy will set it into universal freedom. But there must be a renunciation or letting go of old thoughts before the new can find place in the consciousness. This is a psychological law, which has its outer expression in the intricate eliminative functions of the body.

As the physiologist studies the body, so the metaphysician studies the mind. It is true that some metaphysicians are not careful students. They often jump to conclusions, just as the ancient physiologists made wild guesses about the character of the bodily organs; but the majority of those who work with the inner forces get an understanding that conforms in fundamentals to the discoveries of other metaphysicians in the same field of work. The careful modern metaphysician does not arrive at his conclusions through speculation; he analyzes and experiments with the operations of his own mind until he discovers laws that govern mind action universally.

All those who go deep enough into the study of the mind agree perfectly on fundamentals, one of which is that the universe originated in mind, was projected into action by thought, and is being sustained by mind power. Self-analysis reveals the manner in which the individual mind acts, and this action is the key to all action in the small and the great, in the microcosm and the macrocosm, in man and in God. Another point of agreement is that thoughts are things, that they are ideas projected into form, partaking of the nature of the thinker.

Metaphysicians make a sharp distinction between the realm of ideas, which is Spirit, and the realm of thought, which is mind. Thoughts act in a realm just above, around, and within the material. They have but one degree more of freedom than matter. Thoughts have a four-dimensional capacity, while things have but three. Yet thoughts are limited to the realm in which they function, and man's consciousness, being made up of thoughts, is of like character. Thus it is possible to overload the mind, as one overloads the stomach. Thoughts must be digested in a manner similar to the way in which food is digested. An eagerness to gain knowledge without proper digestion and assimilation ends in mental congestion. The mind, like the bowels, should be open and free. It is reported that Lyman Beecher said to a friend, whom he was bidding good-by, "Worship God, be even-tempered, and keep your bowels open." It is found by metaphysicians that praise and thanksgiving are laxatives of efficiency and that their cleansing work not only frees the mind of egotism but also cleanses the body of effete matter.

Thoughts are things; they occupy space in the mental field. A healthy state of mind is attained and continued when the thinker willingly lets go the old thoughts and takes on the new. This is illustrated by the inlet and the outlet of a pool of water. Stop the inlet, and the pool goes dry. Close the natural outlet, and the pool stagnates, or, like the Dead Sea, it crystallizes its salts until they preserve everything that they touch.

The action of the mind on the body is, in some of its aspects, similar to that of water on the earth. Living old thoughts over and over keeps the inlet of the new thoughts closed. Then begins crystallization—which *materia medica* has named arteriosclerosis. The cause is supposed to be some other disease, such as syphilis, which is classed as one of the most important of the primal causes of arteriosclerosis. Metaphysicians recognize syphilis as secondary in the realm of effects, and they ask, "What causes syphilis?" The cause is the uncontrolled enjoyment of sex sensation without asking or caring to know the object of that function in human consciousness. It would seem that in this respect the animals were under better discipline than men and women.

The enjoyment of the pleasures of sensation without wisdom's control may be compared to riding in a runaway automobile for the pleasure of the swift pace, wholly disregarding the crash that is sure to follow. But to take away man's freedom would delay his attaining the "son of God" degree, which is open to him when he learns to make a lawful use of the attributes of Being; consequently, he must acquire more wisdom and self-control. Tuberculosis, syphilis, cancers, tumors, and the many other ills of the flesh are evidences that nature has been outraged and is protesting and striving to free itself from its unhappy condition.

Every cell of the body is enveloped in soul or thought, and its initial impulse is to conform to the divine-natural law. When this law is not observed by the will of man and cells are reduced to the slavery of lust, they combine with other cells of like condition, and, rather than submit longer to the debased condition, they destroy the organism. But the destruction of the cell as matter does not destroy it on the mental plane; the mental entity survives, and again seeks to carry out the great law of soul evolution that was implanted in it from the beginning. Thus the repeated incarnations of the soul— not only of the soul cell but of the great aggregation of cells known as man—are found to be a fact that explains the continuity of traits of mind and body handed down from generation to generation. It is not in the flesh that we inherit, but in the thoughts of the flesh. The flesh has returned to dust, but its memories endure until a higher mind power cleanses and lifts them to purer states of consciousness.

It is related in Genesis that when fleeing from the cities of Sodom and Gomorrah, which God was destroying, Lot's wife looked back, and "became a pillar of salt." Salt is a preservative, corresponding to memory. When we remember the pleasures of the senses and long for their return, we preserve or "salt" the sense desire. This desire will manifest somewhere, sometime, unless the memory is dissolved through renunciation. The desire for sensation in the flesh in one incarnation may be expressed in the next in a strong desire for personal love. Having become subconscious, it works in the sub-centers of the organism in a fever of anxiety to attain its object, and it may be named consumption, or some other cell-consuming disease.

Modern medical science has traced nearly all the ills of the body to micro-organisms. The popular remedy is to introduce into the body germs much like the disease germs but of weakened power. The body, thereupon, in self-defense generates in the blood stream that which counteracts or neutralizes the disease and renders the body immune to severe attack. If the patient is to continue to be immune, it logically follows that he must continue to have the disease germs in his system, because if they should desert him he would again be open to attack. Typhoid fever is quieted, or forestalled, by turning loose in the system good-natured typhoid germs. But the cause is not removed, and some who follow up such cases say that serums are spreading various forms of disease, and in various ways making the human family less virile. The writer knows of one instance where a healthy boy was vaccinated. A few months later he was attacked by tuberculosis of the hip, which the doctors said was caused by impure blood. All of this goes to show that the right kind of serum has not yet been discovered by medical science and that diseases are not cured by serums but are merely diverted, and eventually break out in other forms.

We see that such bacteriologists as Koch and

Pasteur have merely a clue to the real serum, which is the new life stream opened to man by Jesus Christ. It is true that the bodies of men are being destroyed by disease germs and that the palliative methods of bacteriology may enable us to live a little longer in the body, but until the Christ remedy is applied no real healing has been done. Destructive germs are the creations of destructive thoughts, and until the specific thought is found, physicists will continue to search for the healing serum. Their search is evidence that such a serum exists.

Destructive thinking separates soul and body, and, when the separation is complete, bacteria take up the work and distribute the body wreckage over the earth. If the body were left intact, this planet would soon become the abode of mummies, and the dead would crowd out the living. Then, so long as people continue to die, it is well that microbes make their bodies of some use.

> Imperious Caesar, dead and turn'd to clay,
> Might stop a hole to keep the wind away.

When the body becomes locally infested with bacterial thoughts and separates from the higher Self, a forced removal of the adverse colony, by surgery, sometimes gives at least temporary relief. Man is the dominant thinking and character-giving force of the earth, and he has made it a place of desolation when it should be a paradise. Because of his lust, anger, arrogance, and ignorance, man has been tormented by pests, storms, and earthquakes.

Tradition says that in the dim past this planet's mental atmosphere was charged with the thoughts of men and women who exercised the power of mind in lust, arrogance, and ambition until extreme measures had to be resorted to by the planetary God.

This story (which is merely a legend) relates that perversion of nature and her innocent life energies began cycles ago, when man in the first exuberance of psychic power built up a priestly hierarchy in the ancient continent of Atlantis. These masters of black magic dominated the world and dispossessed the cosmic mind. Extraordinary measures of safety for the whole race became necessary, and the higher powers planned and carried out the destruction of the continent Atlantis and all its people. The very soil of the continent which these occultists occupied had become saturated with lust and selfishness, and it was condemned as unfit to remain a part of the parent planet. The corrupted soil was scooped out of what is now the Atlantic Ocean and thrown off into space, where it became the lifeless mass known as the moon. The earth reeled like a drunkard under this terrible surgical operation, and still wabbles out of true perpendicular, the result of the shock and of the removal of so large a part of its body. Before this catastrophe occurred, a tropical climate extended to the very poles. The remains of tropical plants and animals are found in the frigid zones today, mute evidences that a great and sudden change has at some time taken place in the planet's relation to the sun. The withdrawal of warmth from the poles resulted

in an unnatural coldness that congealed rain into
snow and ice, which slowly piled up at the poles
until they capped the earth to a great depth. This
brought about the great glacial period, which
lasted thousands of years, a reminder of which we
get in icy blasts from the north, with months of
cold and snow. However, the earth is slowly regain-
ing its equilibrium and will in due season be restored to its pristine golden age, and all the desert
places will bloom as the rose. So runs the tradition.

But how about the states of consciousness that
man has built up and from which he would be free?
No one can play fast and loose with God. What one
builds one must care for. What man forms that is
evil he must unform before he can take the coveted
step up the mountain of the ideal. Here enters the
factor that dissolves the structures that are no
longer useful; this factor in metaphysics is known as
denial. Denial is not, strictly speaking, an attribute
of Being as principle, but it is simply the absence of
the impulse that constructs and sustains. When the
ego consciously lets go and willingly gives up its
cherished ideals and loves, it has fulfilled the law of
denial and is again restored to the Father's house.

As all desire is fulfilled through the formative
word, so all denial must be accomplished in word or
conscious thought. This is the mental cleansing
symbolized by water baptism. In a certain stage of
his problem, man makes for himself a state of consciousness in which selfishness dominates. Personal
selfishness is merely an excess of self-identity. This

inflation of the ego must cease, that a higher field of action may appear. One who has caught sight of higher things is desirous of making unity with them. That unity must be orderly and according to the divine procession of mind. One who is housed in the intellect through desire may be ushered into the realm of Spirit by zeal. The first step is a willingness to let go of every thought that holds the ego on the plane of sense. This willingness to let go is symbolical of John the Baptist's crying in the wilderness, denying himself the luxuries of life, living on locusts and wild honey, and wearing skins for clothing.

The personalities of Scripture represent mental attitudes in the individual. John the Baptist and the Pharisees symbolize different phases of the intellect. John is willing to give up the old and is advocating a general denial through water baptism— mental cleansing. The Pharisees cling to tradition, custom, and Scripture, and refuse to let go. John represents the intellect in its transition from the natural to the spiritual plane. The Pharisees have not entered this transition, but cling to the old and defend it by arguments and Scripture quotations. Jesus, who represents the spiritual consciousness, does not take the Pharisees into account as a link in His chain, but of John He says: "Among them that are born of women there hath not arisen a greater than John the Baptist: yet he that is but little in the kingdom of heaven is greater than he." Jesus recognizes that the mental attitude represented by John is a prophecy of greater things, in fact the most desirable mental condition for the intellect on its way to attainment, yet not to be compared with the mental state of those who have actually come into the consciousness of Spirit.

Every man who cries out for God is John the Baptist crying in the wilderness. You who are satiated with the ways of the flesh man, and are willing to give up his possessions and pleasures, are John. The willingness to sacrifice the things of sense starts you on the road to the higher life, but you do not begin to taste its sweets until you actually give up consciously the sense things that your heart has greatly desired.

There are many phases of this passing over from John to Jesus, and some involve unnecessary hardships. The ascetic takes the route of denial so energetically that he starves his powers instead of transforming them. Some Oriental suppliants for divine favor castigate their flesh in many ways, starve their bodies, slash their flesh, and then salt it; they maltreat the body until it becomes a piece of inanimate clay that the soul can vacate until the birds build their nests in the hair of its head. This is Oriental denial, atrophy of the senses. Some Occidental metaphysicians are trying to imitate these agonizing methods of discipline, but in the mind rather than in the body.

John the Baptist stands for the mental attitude that believes that because the senses have fallen into ignorant ways, they are bad and should be killed out. There is a cause for every mental tangent, and that which would kill the sense man, root and branch, has the thought of condemnation as its point of departure from the line of harmony. In John it seemed a virtue, in that he condemned his own errors, but this led to his condemnation of Herod, through which he lost his head. We learn from this that condemnation is a dangerous practice from any angle.

The intellect is the Adam man that eats of the tree of good and evil. Its range of observation is limited, and it arrives at its conclusions by comparison. It juggles with two forces, two factors—positive and negative, good and evil, God and Devil. Its conclusions are the result of reasoning based on comparison, hence limited. The intellect, judging by appearances, concludes that existence is a thing to be avoided. The intellect, beholding the disaster and the misery wrought by the misuse of men's passions, decides that they should be crushed out by starvation. This is the origin of asceticism, the killing out, root and branch, of every appetite and passion, because in the zeal of action they have gone to excess.

Yet John the Baptist has a very important office in the development of man from intellectual to spiritual consciousness. As Jesus said:

"This is he, of whom it is written,

Behold, I send my messenger before thy face,

Who shall prepare thy way before thee."

Thus John the Baptist is the forerunner of Spirit. He stands for the perception of Truth which prepares the way for Spirit through a letting go of narrow beliefs, and a laying hold of divine ideas.

The beliefs that you and your ancestors have held in mind have become thought currents so strong that their course in you can be changed only by your resolute decision to entertain them no longer. They will not be turned out unless the ego through whose domain they run decides positively to adopt means of casting them out of his consciousness, and at the same time erects gates that will prevent their inflow from external sources. This is done by denial and affirmation; the denial always comes first. The John the Baptist attitude must begin the reformation. Man must be willing to receive the cleansing of Spirit before the Holy Ghost will descend upon him. Whoever is not meek and lowly in the presence of Spirit is not yet ready to receive its instruction.

This obedient, receptive state means much to him who wants to be led into the ways of the supreme good. It means that he must have but one source of life, one source of Truth, and one source of instruction; he must be ready to give up every thought that he has imbibed in this life, and must be willing to begin anew, as if he had just been born into the world a little, ignorant, innocent babe. This means so much more than people usually conceive that it dawns on the mind very slowly.

All who sincerely desire the leading of Spirit acquiesce readily in the theoretical statement of the necessity of humility and childlikeness, but when it comes to the detailed demonstration, many are nonplused. This is just as true among metaphysicians as among orthodox Christians. Spirit will find a way to lead you when you have freely and fully dedicated yourself to God, and you will be led in a path just a little different from that of anyone else. Your teaching has been in generalities, so when Spirit in its office as an individual guide shows you Truth different from that which you have been taught, you may object. If, for instance, you have been taught to ignore the body with all its passions and appetites, and Spirit in its instruction shows you that you are to recognize these appetites and passions as your misdirected powers, what are you going to do about it?

There can be but one course for the obedient devotee. If you have surrendered all to omnipresent wisdom, you must take as final what it tells you. You will find that its guidance is that right course for you and, in the end, that it was the only course that you could possibly have taken.

All things are manifestations of the good. Man in his spiritual identity is the very essence of good, and he can do no wrong. He can in his experience misuse the powers placed at his disposal by the Father, but he can do no permanent evil. He always has recourse to Spirit, which forgives all his transgressions and places him on the right road, a new man, when he willingly gives up his own way and as a little child asks to be led. Then comes the redemption of the appetites and passions, which the ignorant intellect has pronounced evil and has attempted to kill out by starvation and repression. This does not mean that the indulgence of appetites and passions is to be allowed in the old, demoralizing way, but it means that they are to be trained anew under the direction of Spirit.

John the Baptist represents the attitude of spiritual receptivity that awaits the higher way as a little child awaits the helping hand of a parent. It is not the arbitrary disciplinarian, but the loving, tender kindergarten teacher that illustrates in visible life the intricate problems that perplex the mind. When man is receptive and obedient, giving himself unreservedly up to Spirit and to receiving its guidance without antagonism, he is delighted with the possibilities that are disclosed to him in the cleansing of mind and body. He then begins to realize what Jesus meant when He said: "If any man would come after me, let him deny himself, and take up his cross, and follow me."

The cross is not a burden, as commonly understood, but is a symbol of the forces in man adjusted in their right relation. The body of Jesus was lifted up and nailed to the cross, which indicates that the physical man must be lifted into the harmony of Spirit and adjusted to its four-dimensional plane, represented by the four branches of the crosstree.

Man thinks in the fourth dimension, but his body, in its present fleshly consciousness, can express in three dimensions only. Hence we must cleanse our thoughts by denying materiality. Then the flesh will become radiant ether with power to penetrate all so-called material substance. But before this can be done the mind of the man must become John the

Baptist—it must be cleansed by the waters of denial, and the old material ideas must be put away forever.

If you are clinging to any idea that in any way prevents your eyes from seeing the millennium here and now, you are a Pharisee; you are crying, "Beelzebub," whenever you say "crank" of the one who has caught sight of the spiritual mountaintops now glistening in the sun of the new age.

John the Baptist is now moving swiftly among the children of men. His cry is heard in many hearts today, and they are following him in the wilderness of sense. But the bright light of the Christ still shines in Galilee, and they who are earnest and faithful shall see it and be glad.

Those who attempt to heal the body by injecting into it a new life stream from without are attempting to do in a material way what Jesus attained spiritually. The vitality of the race was at a low ebb at His advent; He saw the necessity of a larger consciousness of life, and He knew how to inoculate the mind of everyone who would accept His method. In John 5:26 it is written, "For as the Father hath life in himself, even so gave he to the Son also to have life in himself." Life is spiritual, as everyone admits who has tried to find it in a physical laboratory. No one has even seen life in food or drink, but it is there in small degree, and it is through eating and drinking that the body absorbs the invisible life elements that physical science has named vitamins. The vitamin is the essential life within all forms and, being spiritual in character, must be spiritually discerned. We feel life's thrill in our body; by raising this consciousness of life to Christ enthusiasm, we may come to such fullness of energy that the whole life stream will be quickened and the congestions in arteries and glands swept away. "I came that they may have life, and may have *it* abundantly."

All spiritual metaphysicians know that the body and the blood of Jesus were purified and that each cell was energized with original spiritual substance and life, until all materiality was purged away and only the pure essence remained. This vitamin, or essence of life and substance, was sown as seed in the whole race consciousness, and whoever through faith in Christ draws to himself one of these life germs becomes inoculated to that degree with Jesus Christ quality, and not only the mind but also the body is cleansed.

"He that soweth the good seed is the Son of man; and the field is the world." Like a seed planted in soil, the word or thought germ will multiply and bring forth after its kind. "He that abideth in me, and I in him, the same beareth much fruit: for apart from me ye can do nothing."

The apostle Thaddaeus, called also Lebbaeus, carries forward the work of elimination of error thoughts from the mind and of waste food from the body.

The nerve center from which the eliminative function directs the emptying of the intestines is located deep in the lower bowels.

This center is very sensitive to thoughts about

substance and all materiality. A gripping mental hold on material things will cause constipation. A relaxation of the mind and a loosening of the grip on material possessions will bring about freedom in bowel action.

The prevailing ills of the abdominal region, constipation, tumors, and the like, are caused by constriction of the whole body energy.

The faculties centering in the head are responsible for this slowing down of the life forces. The will, operating through the front brain, controls the circulation of the life force in the whole organism. A tense will, set to accomplish some personal end, keys everything to that end and puts a limitation on the activity of every other function.

The set determination to succeed in some chosen field of action, study, profession, business, or personal ambition calls most of the body energy to the head and starves the other centers.

In our schools the minds of our children are crammed with worldly wisdom, and they are spurred on to make their grades, thus constantly forcing the blood to the head and depleting its flow to the abdomen.

This overflow to the will center causes enlarged adenoids, inflamed tonsils, sinus trouble, and other ills of the head, while the abdominal region suffers with constipation and general lack of vital action. Some persons relax in sleep and thus give the body an opportunity to recoup its depleted energy. But if the eager pace is kept up night and day, the end is nervous prostration. The remedy is relaxation of will, the letting go of personal objectives.

The strife to get on in the world is responsible for most of the ills of the flesh. Worry or anxiety about temporal needs disturbs in the body the even flow of nature's all-providing elements. Jesus warned against the tension of anxiety when He said, "Be not anxious for your life, what ye shall eat, or what ye shall drink; nor yet for your body, what ye shall put on. Is not the life more than the food, and the body than the raiment?"

A divine law has been provided for man that will meet every need when it is observed: "Seek ye first his kingdom, and his righteousness; and all these things shall be added unto you."

So we find that relaxation of the tense abdomen depends on relaxation of the tense will. Give up your willfulness and ask that the divine will be done in you and in all your affairs. Jesus set aside His will that God's will might be done in Him. "Not my will, but thine, be done."

CHAPTER 13

Generative Life

THE LAW of generation is undoubtedly the mystery of mysteries in human consciousness. Men have probed, with more or less success, nearly every secret of nature, but of the origin of life they know comparatively nothing. It is true that they have with chemical combinations simulated life, but the activity has been temporary only.

In the phenomenal world, life is the energy that propels all forms to action. Life in the body is like electricity in a motor. As the engineer directs and regulates the electricity in a motor, so the life in the body has its engineer. Life is not in itself intelligent—it requires the directive power of an entity that knows where and how to apply its force, in order to get the best results. The engineer of the life force in the body of man is the life ego; this is the consciousness of life in the organism.

The life ego is the most subtle and most variable of all the powers of man. It is an animal force, and is designated in the Bible allegory as one of the "beasts of the field." It presides over the life and generative function of the body, and because of its tendency to separate and segregate itself from the other bodily functions, it is called the "adversary." It is not essentially evil, but because of its place as the central pole of all bodily activity, its tendency is to centralize all action around its consciousness.

In its divine-natural relation, the life ego has its positive pole in the top head, which is the "heaven" of man's consciousness. When the personality gets active and begins to exercise in the higher or spiritual forces, the life ego becomes inflated with its own importance and falls from heaven (top head) to earth, or front brain. When the seventy whom Jesus had indued with spiritual power returned, they proclaimed that even the demons were subject to them. Then Jesus said, "I beheld Satan as lightning fall from heaven." Jesus was evidently quoting Isaiah, who wrote in the fourteenth chapter of his book (King James Version):

"How art thou fallen from heaven, O Lucifer, son of the morning! *how* art thou cut down to the ground, which didst weaken the nations!

For thou hast said in thine heart, I will ascend into heaven, I will exalt my throne above the stars of God: I will sit also upon the mount of the congregation, in the sides of the north:

I will ascend above the heights of the clouds; I will be like the most High.

Yet thou shalt be brought down to hell, to the sides of the pit."

Jesus warned the seventy not to rejoice over their spiritual power and added, "But rejoice that your names are written in heaven."

In order to give man a body having life in itself, God had to endow him with a focal life center, located in the generative organs. This center of activity in the organism is also the seat of sensation, which is the most subtle and enticing of all factors that enter into being. But these qualities (sensation and generation) were necessary to man's character, and without them he would not have been the complete representative, or image and likeness, of God.

God does not tempt man to break His law, but a great creative plan is being worked out in which the Deity is incarnating itself in its creation. This incarnation is called the Son of man; in man a wonderful being is in process of creation. This being is spiritual man, who will be equal with God, when he overcomes, or handles with wisdom and power, the faculties of the body. The body is the Garden of Eden.

What metaphysicians most need is a comprehension of the factors that go to make up consciousness. This requires discrimination, judgment, and self-analysis.

We talk glibly about God as life, love, intelligence, and substance, and about man as His manifestation, but when we come to describe that manifestation we "lump it off" as the product of thought. What we now need to know is how thought groups the different attributes of Being, for on this combination depends the bringing forth of the ideal man.

We must learn to watch our consciousness, its impulses and desires, as the chemist watches his solutions. Man forms his own consciousness from the elements of God, and he alone is responsible for the results.

Consciousness is a deep subject, and to go into it exhaustively would require the writing of many books. Concisely stated, three great factors enter into every consciousness—intelligence, life, substance. The harmonious combination of these factors requires the most careful attention of the ego, because it is here that all the discords of existence arise.

In Scripture the divine life combined with divine substance is termed "the Lamb of God." This phrase carries the symbology of the Lamb's purity, innocence, and guilelessness. Its nature is to vivify with perpetual life all things that it touches. It knows only to give, give unceasingly and eternally, without restraint. It does not carry wisdom; that is another quality of Being, which man comprehends from a different part of his consciousness.

The pure life of God flows into man's consciousness through the spiritual body, and is sensed by the physical at a point in the loins. This is the "river of water of life, bright as crystal, proceeding out of the throne of God and of the Lamb," referred to in the twenty-second chapter of Revelation.

Only those who have come into consciousness of the spiritual body can feel this holy stream of life. When the ego has found it, and laved in its cleansing currents, the ecstasy of Elysian realms is experienced. It cannot be described, because all the sensations of the mortal consciousness are coarse, compared with its transcendent sweetness and purity.

Many feel its thrills in part in silent meditation or in religious enthusiasm and are temporarily stimulated by its exquisite vibrations. Just here is where the danger lies for those who have not brought out the other pole of Being—intelligence.

The ego, through its recognition of this life stream, sets it flowing to every faculty. Being by nature formless, the life stream takes the mold and character of that into which it is poured. It is the servant of the ego, the *I*, which man is, and through his failure to recognize the divine intelligence, which should show him how to use it in the right way, he blunders ahead in his ignorance, and the Lamb of God is slain from the foundation of the world.

The greatest danger of perversion lies in the direction of the carnal thought of sex, because it is there that this pure stream has been most foully polluted by ignorance. Sex sensation has made a broken cistern of man's consciousness; for generations the life stream has been turned into this receptacle, and lust has robbed the bodies of the whole race, making them mere shells, void of life. The failing eye, the deaf ear, the festering of withering flesh, all bear testimony to this perversion of God's life.

Yet men and women, otherwise applying good reason, continue their lustful practices and at the same time wonder why God does not give them more life.

They run here and there, seeking a restoring elixir for their failing powers; they call on God for help, while they continue to squander His energy in lust.

Man is male and female, which are qualities of mind—love and wisdom. Every attempt to lower these divine attributes to the physical plane meets with disaster. It has been tried again and again in every age, and its votaries have always gone into demoralization if they persisted in trying to carry out their theories.

Yet it is not unlawful to have bodily sensations in regeneration. A change in ideas must necessarily produce a change in the body, and there is a perfect response in every center of consciousness when Spirit has been welcomed as the rightful inhabitant of the body. The marriage mystically spoken of in Scripture, and in other sacred books, takes place in the consciousness; it is a soul communion of the two-in-one, more sweet than that between the most harmoniously mated man and woman. This eliminates sex in its outer manifestation.

Persistently deny the carnal belief in sex, and realize that the life stream, which has been turned outward and named "sex," is not of that character in its original purity, but is pure spiritual life.

You must cleanse this pure stream in its outward flow by destroying the carnal sense of sex. This can be done only by the power of your word. Do not kill out the life manifesting through your body by denying it away entirely; deny away the sense of impurity with which the animal ego has clothed it.

"To the pure all things are pure" does not mean that lasciviousness is pure, nor that the deifying of sexuality is pure. The purity is in knowing that behind and interior to these shadows is a pure substance that is of God, that must be seen by the eye of the pure. So long as your eye sees sex and the indulgence thereof, on any of its planes, you are not pure. You must become so mentally translucent that you see men and women as sexless beings—which they are in the spiritual consciousness.

Sex lust is the father of death. James, in the first chapter of his epistle, gives its history in these words: "Then the lust, when it hath conceived, beareth sin: and the sin, when it is fullgrown, bringeth forth death."

Paul says, "To be carnally minded *is* death" (KJV), and Jesus, in the twelfth chapter of Mark, sums up the whole question in these words: "For when they shall rise from the dead [come out of the carnal consciousness], they neither marry, nor are given in marriage; but are as angels in heaven."

To desire to be instructed by God is the first step in exalting the inner life force. The sincere desire of the heart is always fulfilled by the divine law. All the woes of humanity have their root in disregard of law. Man has to deal with many factors in his "garden." The most "subtle" is the "serpent," or sense consciousness. It is not evil, as we have been taught to believe. The allegory given in the third chapter of Genesis plainly teaches that sensation (serpent) is a blind force, which should not be regarded as a source of wisdom. In its right relation the serpent stands upright on its tail and forms the connecting link between the swift vibratory forces of Spirit and the slow vibrations of the flesh. "As Moses lifted up the serpent in the wilderness, even so must the Son of man be lifted up." In the body the spinal cord is the main cable of sensation, "the tree . . . in the midst of the garden," and its branches extend to all parts of the system. The "fruit" of this "tree," which the desire for sensation (serpent) urges man to eat, is the seminal fluid, which flows throughout the nervous system and is the connecting link between the mind and the body. When desire for sensation leads man to dissipate (eat) this precious "fruit" of the "tree" in his earthly garden, the whole nervous system is drained of its vitality and the spinal cord loses its capacity to conduct the higher life into the consciousness. Man feels a lack; he is "naked." Sensation is no longer a heavenly ecstasy but a fleshly sex vibration. It crawls on its "belly" and eats "dust" all the days of its life; that is, it functions in the driest, most lifeless part of man's being.

Yet sensation is a divine creation; it is part of the Lord God's formation and must find expression somewhere in the consciousness. This brings us to the root cause of that appetite which craves stimulants and goes to excess in seeking satisfaction in eating and in drinking. The cause is plainly to be seen when we understand the anatomy of mind and body. Sensation is seeking satisfaction through the appetites. By listening to this serpent of sense, man becomes sexually insane, a glutton and a drunkard.

The remedy is this: Turn away from the lusts of the flesh and seek God. Take up the problem from its spiritual standpoint. Sensation is a mental quality. It can be satisfied only by cultivation of the spiritual side of the nature. If you are a sexual drunkard, deny the power of this ungodly lust over you. Pray for the help to overcome, then affirm your own power and spiritual dominion over all the "beasts of the field" in your "garden." When you have obtained mastery over sexual intemperance, you will find the conquest of appetite easy. Simply deny all desire for material stimulants and affirm that you are satisfied with the stimulant of Spirit. Whenever the desire for the material stimulant manifests itself, say to it: *You are nothing. You have no power over me or over anybody else. I am Spirit, and I am wholly satisfied by the great flood of spiritual life that now fills my being.*

The result of sin is death; the truth of these words has been proven for ages. But when he was tempting her to disobey the divine law, the "adversary" said to Eve, "Ye shall not surely die." The tragedy of Eden is being enacted every day in every individual of the race, and death reigns in consequence. We may call it by any other name, but the breaking up of consciousness and the separation of Spirit, soul, and body take place just the same. As Emerson said, "Behold a god in ruins." In face of the facts that God pronounced death to be the wages of sin and that the experience of the race has proved His words true, many people have listened to the "adversary" and have believed his lie. We hear them on every side saying, "Ye shall not surely die."

As the result of sin the whole human race is already "dead in trespasses and sins"; that is, the race is in a dying condition, which ends in the loss of the body. Death is not annihilation, because a resurrection has been promised.

To be "dead in trespasses and sins" is to lack realization of God, to be ignorant of His law and disobedient to it. When Jesus said, "I am the resurrection, and the life," He was telling of the power of the Christ Mind to enter the mind and the body of man as quickening Spirit to awaken the whole consciousness to the knowledge of God. This resurrecting process is now going on in many people. It is a gradual change that brings about a complete transformation of the body through renewal of the mind. Spirit, soul, and body become unified with Christ Mind, and body and soul become immortal and incorruptible. In this way death is overcome.

Those who insist that men do not die as a result of sin are building up a false hope of finding life after death. Those who understand that eternal life has been lost to the race through sin, and can be regained only through the resurrecting power of the Christ Mind in the individual, are building on the eternal foundation of Truth. Everyone must at some time come to understand that this statement is absolutely true: "He that hath the Son [consciousness of Christ] hath the life; he that hath not the Son of God hath not the life."

The belief that all the entities that speak through mediums are the spirits of dead people is not proved. The communications are so fragmentary, and usually so inferior to the natural ability of the supposed egos delivering them, that those of wide investigation doubt the authenticity of the authorship. No great literary production, great scientific discovery, or great sermon has ever come from spirits, yet the country in which it is claimed that they exist should contain all the wise people who have lived on the earth.

This theory of continuous progressive life after death contradicts the teachings of the Bible. God did not create man to die; death is the result of a transgression of law. Christianity teaches that man was created to live in his body, refining it as his thoughts unfold, and that the work of the Christ— the supermind in man—is to restore this state; that is, unite Spirit, soul, and body here on earth. This must be fulfilled in the whole race, and every thought of death, or the possibility of leaving the body, must be put out of the mind.

Practical Christians object to thoughts that tend to separate soul and body, because by such thoughts is built up a consciousness that finally brings about that dissolution. It is a fact, well known to those who have deeply studied the law of Being, that death does separate Spirit, soul, and body; that the communications received by spiritualists are but echoes of the soul, without its animating, inspiring, spiritual I AM; that this mentality that communicates falls in its turn into a sleep, or coma, even as the body does, until the law again brings about a union with its I AM or higher Self and the building of another physical organism takes place. This process of repeated body building by the ego continues until the man, through Christ, makes a complete union of Spirit, soul, and body here on earth. This union brings all of man's powers into conjunction, and what is mystically known as the Jesus Christ man, or redeemed man, appears.

We can easily see how illogical, unwise, and futile it is to teach that man can lay off his body as a worn-out garment and, by weakly giving up and dying, go on to higher attainment. We know whereof we speak, and we must proclaim this great Truth that Jesus taught: "Whosoever liveth and believeth on me [spiritual I AM] shall never die."

If God created man to die and go on to a spirit land to get his education, then it would be better for him to die in infancy and escape the hardships of life. Also, if death is part of God's law, we are defeating the law every time we attempt to escape death by trying to heal the body.

If man's birth as an infant a few years ago was the beginning of his existence, then God has performed a miracle and made an exception of man in the progressive law of development that is evident in all His other works.

The fact is—and it is well known to initiates— that spiritualists are in communication with the mentality of humanity, that is, the personal consciousness. Not having developed the superconscious mind, they do not understand the creative law. They function mentally and physically in a thought psychism that is mixed and uncertain. Their communications can all be explained in the action of the subconscious minds of the living, and the majority of mediums are uncertain as to whether they are moved by their own or some other mentality.

When man has brought his higher Self into action he will see clearly the relation of Spirit, soul, and body, in all phases of their action.

If you want to know all the mysteries of life, study life and put out of your mind every thought about death or the condition of the dead. Then through the law of thought formation you will build up in yourself such a strong consciousness of life that its negative (or absence) will ever be to you nonexistent. Jesus meant this when He said, "If a man keep my word, he shall never see death."

The desire to live does not cease when the body dies. The mind lives on, not in heaven or hell, but in the states of consciousness that it has cultivated in life. Mind does not change with a change of environment. Those who leave the body of matter find themselves in a body of ether, which does not respond to their desire for coarse sensations. Jesus taught in Luke 16:23 that the rich man who died was in "torment" in Hades. In the original language in which the Bible was written *Hades* was a term used to represent the unseen world. Those who have cultivated spiritual thoughts find themselves at death in an environment and in an ether body corresponding to their prevailing thoughts. But the very fact that they died proves that they gave up to the "adversary," that they did not attain the dominion, power, and authority of spiritual man. Consequently after a period of recreation and rest they will again take up active, overcoming life in a flesh body through reincarnation. So this process of life and death will continue until the ego overcomes sin, sickness, and death, and raises the body of flesh to the body of Spirit without the tragedy of death. "This corruptible must put on incorruption; this mortal must put on immortality."

Our theologians have not discerned man's life in its entirety—they have attempted to crowd into one physical incarnation the character that it has taken aeons to develop. As taught by Jesus, and by all spiritual teachers, the goal of man is the attainment of eternal life, the overcoming of physical death. The human race on this planet will continue to die and be reborn until it learns the law of right living, which will ultimate in a body so healthy that it will never die. Jesus demonstrated this, and He promised those who should follow Him in the regeneration that they would never see death if they should keep His words. Many Christians are getting this understanding—that they have not attained eternal life so long as they allow the body to continue in the corruption that ends in death, and they are earnestly beginning the appropriation, or eating and drinking, of the life and substance of the Lord's body, until He appears again in their regeneration organism.

QUESTION HELPS

For Students of
The Twelve Powers of Man

THE TWELVE POWERS OF MAN
CHAPTER ONE

1. What do Jesus' Twelve Apostles represent in man's spiritual ongoing?

2. What is symbolized by the first and Second Coming of Christ, as spoken of in the Scriptures?

3. How may the Twelve Apostles be likened to the heads of departments in an industrial plant?

4. What does Jesus represent in man's consciousness?

5. Name each apostle and the corresponding faculty represented.

6. Why was Peter (faith) called the first apostle?

7. Explain how a nerve center may be baptized by the word of Spirit and given a new power.

8. Why does the intellect deny that man can have knowledge of God?

9. How should the twelve powers of man be developed and expressed?

THE DEVELOPMENT OF FAITH
CHAPTER TWO

1. What does Abraham represent in man's consciousness?

2. Why must this faculty be abiding?

3. Why is faith put to a test?

4. Give the symbology represented by Abraham's offering of his son Isaac.

5. Explain the law of giving and receiving.

6. What is symbolized by the "upper room" to which the Holy Spirit comes?

7. What is the difference between the prayer of supplication and the affirmative prayer?

8. What are the two attitudes of faith that are brought out? Explain.

9. Who was the first and greatest apostle of Jesus?

10. What does his name mean?

11. Why was his name changed after he became Jesus' apostle?

12. What is the difference between trust and real faith?

13. Why is the spoken word formative, but not always creative?

14. Where is the faith center in the body of man? How is it quickened?

15. What is the significance of a change of mind?

16. Explain how Jesus accomplished the mighty works credited to Him.

STRENGTH—STABILITY—STEADFASTNESS
CHAPTER THREE

1. Which one of Jesus' apostles symbolized strength in man's consciousness?

2. Wherein is the source of all things?

3. Why is man greater than all other expressions of Divine Mind?

4. What is the difference between the Jehovah man and the Adam man?

5. Explain God's creation of man as "male and female."

6. What does the "strong *man* fully armed," referred to by Jesus, represent in the natural man?

7. What does it represent in the regenerate man?

8. Explain the symbology brought out by the story of David and Goliath.

9. What does Samson symbolize in man's consciousness?

10. Explain the symbology of his being robbed of his hair by Delilah.

11. Why should man conserve the vital essence of his body?

12. Explain how one may renew the body through using the various brain centers.

13. How does creative law affect man's development?

14. Explain man's growth in consciousness through evolution.

15. Why is the Word of God likened unto a seed?

16. Why is Jesus Christ the Great Teacher?

WISDOM—JUDGMENT
CHAPTER FOUR

1. What are the twelve powers of man?

2. Where is the wisdom center in man's consciousness?

3. Name some attributes of wisdom.

4. Is knowledge of the negative side of good necessary to man's unfoldment?

5. Explain some of the functions of the solar plexus, and name its presiding ego.

6. What is man's first step in the regeneration?

7. Where is this step referred to in Scripture symbology?

8. How do we "call a disciple"? Give an example.

9. What is Christ?

10. Explain the lawful method of entering the kingdom of God.

11. Can man escape divine judgment? Why?

12. What part does spiritual judgment play in the working out of man's salvation?

13. Why are Peter, James, and John mentioned more than the other apostles?

14. Why was Andrew also among the first-called?

REGENERATING LOVE
CHAPTER FIVE

1. Explain how man may use his creative forces in cooperation with the creative law.

2. What are the "sons of God" in Scripture symbology?

3. How do we know that Being is masculine and feminine?

4. What is the name and nature of God's most beautiful "daughter"?

5. Name some virtues and vices of mother love.

6. Explain love in its role of "gravity."

7. Is love ever a source of misery? Explain.

8. Give a remedy for divorce.

9. What do Adam, Eve, and the serpent symbolize in the individual?

10. Give the metaphysical explanation of Adam and Eve's eating of the fruit of the tree of the "knowledge of good and evil."

11. What place has love in the regeneration of man?

12. By what means can woman help to lift up man and free him from sense bondage?

13. Will incarnation cease when love is lifted up?

14. What was Jesus' mission on earth?

15. Where is the throne of love in man's spiritual body?

16. Who among Jesus' apostles personified love?

17. Give an original illustration of how unselfish love may be unfolded.

18. Should one employ force or suppression in soul unfoldment? Why?

POWER—DOMINION—MASTERY
CHAPTER SIX

1. What is essential to the realization and demonstration of spiritual power?

2. Over what should man exercise his divine birthright of power?

3. Locate the throne of power in man's body consciousness, and tell which apostle represents power.

4. What effect has development of power on the voice?

5. How and to what extent are one's words imbued with power?

6. Can we overcome the belief in limited or declining power? How?

7. Should man develop power before he overthrows carnal selfishness in himself? Why?

8. How can we distinguish between right and wrong in the use of our power?

9. What is the key to the exercising of dominion successfully in the material world and the restoring of equilibrium between Spirit and matter?

10. What rule did Jesus lay down as the basis of world peace and prosperity?

11. When will the "new heaven and . . . new earth" appear?

12. What is involved in overcoming the world, the flesh, the Devil, and even death?

13. What is the Devil?

14. Give the metaphysical interpretation of the Crucifixion.

15. What is the acme of man's power and dominion?

THE WORK OF THE IMAGINATION IN REGENERATION

CHAPTER SEVEN

1. What is the imagination?

2. Which apostle represents the imagination?

3. Within man what office has the imaging faculty?

4. Why were Jesus' ideas so powerful and enduring?

5. What is the key to the interpretation of symbols?

6. What determines the character of soul and body?

7. Do dreams and visions play an important part in man's soul development? Explain why, and give Scripture examples.

8. Interpret spiritually Peter's vision which is described in the tenth chapter of Acts.

9. What does man's body represent? Explain why.

10. Why do individuals and nations sometimes revert from culture to savagery?

11. How should man handle the animal propensities in himself?

12. Does the fact that animals are good in their rightful place justify man's using them for food? Why?

13. How was the original creation given character and form?

14. What, potentially, are animals?

15. When will animals cease to be in the objective?

UNDERSTANDING

CHAPTER EIGHT

1. Do wisdom, understanding, knowledge, and intelligence all mean the same thing?

2. Explain the two great realms of mind.

3. Was Jesus scientific in His teaching?

4. What faculty of mind is given first place by those who have spiritual discernment?

5. What phase of mind comes first in soul development?

6. What does Solomon stand for?

7. What did the Lord also give unto Solomon because He was so well pleased with him?

8. What part does the heart play in soul unfoldment?

9. Why do we have to be careful in distinguishing between true inspiration and our intellectual reasoning?

10. What does John the Baptist stand for in man's consciousness?

11. Who did Jesus say John the Baptist had been?

12. What takes place in man when he gives himself wholly unto the Lord?

13. Explain the relationship between John the Baptist and Jesus.

14. How does this relationship apply to man's consciousness?

15. What is the greatest of all the powers of man?

16. Do all the faculties enter into the regeneration of man?

17. Does man have the privilege of attaining eternal life?

THE WILL IS THE MAN
CHAPTER NINE

1. What faculty of mind is the motive power for all the other faculties?

2. What other faculty is most closely related to it?

3. What part does the imagination play in the development of the soul?

4. Why has man been given free will?

5. What is the work of the solar plexus?

6. How do the will and the understanding conflict in the expression of the spiritual life?

7. What causes hardening of the arteries?

8. Where does "motive" come in?

9. Explain what is meant by man's partaking of the knowledge of good and evil.

10. What does Jesus represent in soul development?

11. How does the Christ discipline His apostles (faculties)?

12. Explain how the will is often allowed to become destructive.

13. What is the will of Divine Mind for man as regards his actions?

14. Explain why a person should be positive in submitting his will to the authority of God instead of doing so in a negative way.

15. With what power and authority did Jesus endow His disciples to go forth and preach?

16. Does God's will for man change?

17. Why do sin, sickness, suffering, and death come into man's life?

18. Should a person submit his will to the control of another? Explain.

19. How should a person make his affirmations?

20. Give the words of Jesus that may be used as an affirmation in bringing about relaxation, peace, and harmony.

———————

SPIRITUAL LAW AND ORDER
CHAPTER TEN

1. For what did Jesus denounce the scribes and Pharisees?

2. Should teachers or leaders frame rules of thought and action for their members? Why?

3. What did Jesus lay down as the only safe foundation for all religious work?

4. Why did Jesus break the Mosaic law?

5. What does the Sabbath day stand for in man's consciousness?

6. Explain why Jesus said that He came not to break the law, but to fulfill it.

7. Why must man erase from his mind all authority and tradition of other men in order to fulfill God's will for him?

8. What place do sacred writings have in man's life?

9. What is the only authority?

10. Shall we leave our fellows free to worship God as they see fit, and to what extent do we co-operate with them?

11. Where does man find real communion with the Father?

12. What part does Jesus, the "only begotten Son" of God, play in man's unfoldment?

13. What does Moses' fleeing to the wilderness represent in man's consciousness? Explain.

14. What gives our words and thoughts power to accomplish that whereto they are sent?

15. What forces do Moses and Pharaoh represent? Explain.

16. Explain the place of denial and affirmation in man's growth.

ZEAL—ENTHUSIASM
CHAPTER ELEVEN

1. What is the function of the ego in forming mental states of consciousness? Explain.

2. What is zeal?

3. Can the divine law be broken? Explain.

4. Should one suppress the impulse of zeal that wells up in consciousness?

5. Why is it necessary for zeal to be tempered with wisdom?

6. How do one's different combinations of thoughts affect soul and body?

7. What is the meaning of the name *Simon Peter?* What is the meaning of the name *Simon, the Cananaean?*

8. Explain how the vitamins in the food that we eat are stored up in body consciousness and liberated.

9. Has zeal any part to play in one's becoming a genius along any line of endeavor?

10. Explain Jesus' words, "The very hairs of your head are numbered."

11. Explain Emerson's words, "Be not deceived by dimples and curls; that child is a thousand years old."

12. How do you account for Mozart's wonderful ability at the age of four years to play the organ without instruction?

13. Where does the zeal center have its throne of dominion?

RENUNCIATION
CHAPTER TWELVE

1. What is the first step in experiencing conversion?

2. Explain the effect of a change of mind on the body organism.

3. In the process of body renewal, where does renunciation come in?

4. How does the metaphysician arrive at his conclusions concerning mind action?

5. State one big fundamental Truth brought out in the study of mind.

6. Explain the distinction between the realm of ideas and the realm of thought.

7. Explain how thoughts are assimilated by the mind.

8. How does the mind act on the body?

9. Why should wisdom be exercised in the control of the mind?

10. Should man be given his freedom? Explain.

11. How are traits of mind and body handed down from generation to generation?

12. How are these dissolved in memory?

13. Explain medical science's method of combating disease germs.

14. Why has it failed?

15. What is the one healing power? Explain its action.

16. Describe the work of Thaddaeus.

17. What is the cause of constipation? Of tumors? Of the slowing down of the life forces?

18. What is the cause of adenoids? Of inflamed tonsils? Of sinus trouble?

19. How may these ills be avoided?

GENERATIVE LIFE
CHAPTER THIRTEEN

1. What is the life energy?

2. Is life intelligence? Explain.

3. Why is the life ego called the "adversary"?

4. Why are sensation and generation necessary to man's character? Explain.

5. What is the Son of man?

6. What does the Garden of Eden symbolize?

7. On what does the bringing forth of the ideal man depend?

8. What three factors enter into every consciousness?

9. What is the Lamb of God? Explain.

10. What is symbolized by the "river of water of life"?

11. Wherein comes the danger in experiencing this holy stream of life?

12. How are bodily sensations lawfully experienced? Explain.

13. Why is it necessary to cleanse this pure stream of life in its flow outward?

14. Explain: "As Moses lifted up the serpent in the wilderness, even so must the Son of man be lifted up."

15. Explain sensation's being a divine creation.

16. How is all intemperance overcome?

17. Explain your being "dead through your trespasses and sins."

INDEX

INDEX

Book Two

CHRIST ENTHRONED IN MAN

by
Cora Dedrick Fillmore

Foreword

These exercises are supplementary to Charles Fillmore's book *The Twelve Powers of Man,* and instruct the readers of that book how to apply the principles therein laid down, and how to awaken within the body, through the action of the mind, the undeveloped or sleeping faculties.

All students of the body temple agree that we are using but a small part of its innate capacity. All students of the mind agree that we are using only a very, very small portion of our mind power. These exercises are for the purpose of developing and bringing into action the wonderful latent possibilities, which will ultimate in a complete union of soul and body. This is the regeneration taught and demonstrated by Jesus Christ.

The Twelve Powers of Man by Charles Fillmore undoubtedly affords the greatest key to logical and rational expression of spiritual man that has ever been given to the public. The adepts of the Orient have in symbol and secret formula revealed to students the possibilities of the soul, and how through years of asceticism and withdrawal from the practical side of life this superperson can be developed.

The advanced scientists of today are recognizing as fundamental truths that mind expresses itself through brain cells and that brain cells, with their nerve aggregations, move the body and the world without. Sir James Jeans, the eminent British scientist, says in substance that it may be that the gods that determine our fate are our own minds working on our brain cells and through them on the world about us.

As the mind incorporates ideas from the one divine source, it enlarges its brain area and gives increased mental and spiritual ability to the whole person. This process continued will transform every cell in the organism into a brain cell, and thus we will be transformed from flesh and blood into the glory of radiant mind. As Jesus Christ was transfigured on the mount before His disciples, so we shall be transfigured in our high understanding and become manifest sons and daughters of God.

The evidence of this palpable truth is found on every side and is now, in *The Twelve Powers of Man* by Mr. Fillmore and in this book of exercises, being scientifically worked out. The fact is that the lives of Jesus Christ and the Twelve Apostles were symbolical demonstrations of the unfoldment of the twelve faculties of man, which we are interpreting in terms of physiology and psychology as cooperating with the supermind of the anointed of God.

All that is necessary is for the student of this book to apply the word given to the body centers as directed chapter by chapter. The results will be a definite transformation of the latent faculties dormant in the so-called physical organism.

The body is composed of trillions of cells, waiting for the mind to stir them into spiritual activity that they may become obedient servants of Christ.

The twelve powers of man, or twelve fundamental faculties of the mind, are represented in Scripture by the twelve sons of Jacob, the Twelve Apostles of Jesus, the twelve gates of the Temple, and many other symbols.

Some metaphysicians have located in the human body twelve dominant brain or nerve centers that correspond with the twelve powers or spiritual faculties. The diagram given at the beginning of the book gives in rough outline the location of these centers, which may be designated as follows:

I AM—Christ—top brain.
Faith—Peter—center of brain.
Strength—Andrew—loins.
Wisdom or Judgment—James, son of Zebedee—pit of stomach.
Love—John—back of heart.
Power—Philip—root of tongue.
Imagination—Bartholomew—between the eyes.
Understanding—Thomas—front brain.
Will—Matthew—center front brain.
Order—James, son of Alphaeus—navel.
Zeal—Simon the Cananaean—back head, *medulla*.
Renunciation or Elimination—Thaddaeus—lower abdominal region.
Life Conserver—Judas—generative function.

CHAPTER 1

⟨⟨⟨⟨⟩⟩⟩⟩

The Centers of Power

"Thy hands have fashioned and made me."
—Job 10:8

Affirmation: *Jesus Christ is now here, raising me to
His super consciousness. I realize that I am the image and
likeness of God, the prism through which Divine Mind
flashes its perfection into expression.*

THERE IS A GREAT deal of agitation about the
development of spiritual-mindedness and what
goes with that development. The general and
popular idea is that some force outside of us is going
to bring about a new race; in other words, that there
is to be a miraculous transformation of the human
family, a transformation wrought by some outer
power through which the higher types of men and
women are to come forth.

There is no warrant for this view in the Scriptures or in the experience of the race. Jesus Christ is
looked upon as the great leader of a new civilization,
and He undoubtedly is. Jesus' and John's opening
declarations were "Repent ye," which means "Change
your mind." So all those who are following Jesus are
finding it necessary gradually to develop out of a

three-dimension consciousness into a four-dimension consciousness, and this is really the transformation named by Jesus "the regeneration."

The exercises in this book show step-by-step how to evolve the natural faculties into the spiritual faculties, and this is what is meant by salvation through Jesus Christ.

In the Resurrection, Jesus manifested Himself in His mental (sometimes called "astral," or psychical) body, but with the spiritual mind dominant. He functioned in this psychical realm for forty days before His ascension. Then through the power of His spiritual nature He raised the psychical body to the spiritual body, which is indestructible, eternal, omnipresent Spirit, one with God. In this experience He blazed a new trail in the omnipresent ether, of which we can all take advantage to enter the royal road that leads to a new spiritual state of consciousness to be enjoyed here and now.

When we have accomplished the process of spiritualizing both soul and body as Jesus accomplished it, we shall be with Him in the kingdom of the heavens—a state of mind in which Spirit, soul, and body are one. Let us look to Jesus as our Way-Shower and Helper.

As Paul said in 1 Corinthians 15:40, 44: "There are celestial bodies and there are terrestrial bodies; but the glory of the celestial is one, and the glory of the terrestrial is another. . . . It is sown a physical body, it is raised a spiritual body. If there is a physical body, there is also a spiritual body."

To each individual, all down the ages, has come

from the still small voice of Spirit within the admonition: "Turn to me and be saved, all the ends of the earth!" That is to say, "Look to the spiritual powers within yourself for your real good." Therefore, in all the exercises that follow, please keep constantly in mind that you are a spiritual being, a god in the making. Let go of all material preconceptions of yourself and dwell continually in the higher dimension, where you see through the eyes of Spirit, hear with the ears of Spirit, and feel with the heart of Spirit.

As we acquaint ourselves with the Almighty and His immutable laws, we think less and less of men and more and more of the greatness of the first great cause, which through Jesus Christ is wooing us to itself. We behold ourselves entering into the inner kingdom of God, perhaps consciously entering at a point just back of the heart and stomach. We see ourselves sitting on a throne and abiding there, our body consciousness being the prism through which His image and likeness is projecting itself more and more into the manifest world.

God, Supreme Being, is the source out of which all creation evolves. God-Mind is an omnipresent spiritual realm comprised of creative ideas. Through prayer and spiritual realization we may lay hold of these ideas, weave them into our soul consciousness, and create out of them the ideals of our hearts.

The soul is the sum total of our thoughts, spiritual and otherwise. Thus we, the masterpiece of Almightiness, have the power to redeem all error thinking and through our words to create our own lives, make our own environment. You and I, the offspring of God-Mind, have the wonderful privilege of forming our lives of God substance, of instilling into our soul and body consciousness the intelligence and energy of the Father, and of shaping our destinies as we will.

The first step after getting the consciousness that you are a spiritual being in both soul and body is to realize that the real I AM entity within each individual functions continuously. The spiritual center, the abode of the Christ, is in the crown of the head; the conscious mind functions through the front forehead; the center of the subconscious mind is in the heart and the abdominal region.

First, centering attention in the crown of the head where we contact superconscious mind, affirm: *The Christ of God is awakening within me.*

As you realize this statement remember that "the Christ" is the perfect-Son idea, containing all wisdom and power.

However, it is not wise to concentrate too intensely at this point for more than a moment or two, at least in the beginning. The power of the word in your realization contacting the superconscious mind naturally causes an outpouring of the Holy Spirit, which is sometimes manifested in a soft, golden light—pure intelligence. Please remember that while the releasing of divine ideas does cause the emanation of a soft, golden light, the emanation of light is useful only as we allow it to dissolve the darkness surrounding us and to expand in our consciousness as pure intelligence. In some instances where a great spiritual realization is being released in consciousness, the light is white and dazzling "as the sun," as recorded in Jesus' experience in the Transfiguration, in Matthew 17:2.

Now allow this Christ light to drop to the front forehead, the seat of the conscious mind. Affirm: *I am aware that the Christ of God is awakening within me.*

At first you may be unaware of the soft, golden light that is descending from the heavens of your mind—which is felt and not seen—but presently you will be able to discern this outpouring as an illumination that gives you new understanding. Then allow the Presence, the Christ light, to drop to the center of the head, the pineal gland. Then declare: *The Christ of God through faith is awakening within me.*

In all the exercises that follow, remember that it is well for the conscious mind, which functions in the front forehead, to be awake to all that is going on and to take cognizance continually of each step in the spiritual unfoldment.

In this connection also please note that the nose is a highly sensitive and intelligent organ. It really symbolizes discernment, and it seems to possess a keen penetrating ability. Be sure the illumination of Spirit is penetrating into this organ and that your discerning powers are quick, keen, energetic.

From that high vantage point, the crown of the head, allow the soft light of Spirit to flow down,

down, penetrating and permeating every function
and cell of soul and body, down even into the hands
and feet. Consciously follow it down into the feet
and even beneath the feet—the heels, especially,
receiving your attention. Here you dwell for some
time, fully aware of the flow of Spirit as pure illumination, awakening in you a greater degree of intelligence from the crown of the head to the soles of
the feet.

With your attention centered in the feet, realize
that the windows of your soul are open toward the
heavens of your mind. In the words of Ella Wheeler
Wilcox:

Let there be many windows to your soul,
That all the glory of the universe
May beautify it. Not the narrow pane
Of one poor creed can catch the radiant rays
That shine from countless sources. Tear away
The blinds of superstition; let the light
Pour through fair windows broad as Truth itself,
And high as God.

Then know that you are saturated in this holy
light, the light of divine intelligence, and that you
are even wrapped about in it, as in a mantle, from
head to feet. This outpouring is known as the descending spiritual current.

By this time you will have discovered that there
is also an ascending current coming up from the
earth. In its original essence this ascending current
was pure substance of Spirit; now, however, it is

tinctured with the race thought that each person must handle. It offers much protection if you realize continually that the descending current of Spirit does make its way entirely through the body temple; that in fact we live in it, move in it, and have our being in it; and that it extends beneath the feet. It contacts the ascending current at various points and tempers and harmonizes all the undisciplined race thoughts of hate, fear, jealousy, lack, and the like. Practice of control of these forces will give you an insight into the Truth that you have the power to use every problem in which you are involved as a stepping-stone to higher achievements. The descending spiritual current and the ascending earthly current, contacting each other at different points in soul and body consciousness, form centers of consciousness, the most important being those in the regions of the heart and stomach and another being the center at the base of the brain, the *medulla*, the zeal center. Minor points of contact are located at other centers.

The activity of divine intelligence in the spiritual flow from above transforms the error beliefs of the race contained in the earthly flow from beneath into constructive forces, and at the same time gives the individual a richer and broader understanding of life in the manifest realm.

The now-transformed constructive flow from beneath continues its upward course, continually contacting the never-ceasing spiritual flow from above. Now consciously you ascend with this up-

ward current to the point that we have already designated as the great distributing nerve center back
of the heart and stomach.

You will find that at this point you have a firm
grip on the power of the word and that the Christ is
setting up a throne of dominion here. In Truth this
is the point where the Lord's body begins to become
manifest (Bethlehem, "house of bread"). Dwelling
consciously here, call down from the heavens of
your mind all the powers—faith, strength, wisdom, love, and so forth. Realize or affirm that these
twelve powers (perfect ideas in God-Mind) are entering the soul consciousness and are organizing
themselves as substance at the very center of being.
Then realize that their substance is being established in the breast and through the whole soul and
body being. You are thus laying the foundation of
the new Christ body or temple of God, with its
twelve precious stones which represent intellectual
perception of the spiritual body. At this point affirm
and realize this invocation: *I am now in the presence of
pure Being, immersed in the Holy Spirit of life, love, and
wisdom. I acknowledge Thy presence and power, O blessed
Spirit. In Thy divine wisdom I now erase my mortal limitations, and from Thy pure substance of love, I bring my
world into manifestation according to Thy perfect law.*

After you have repeated this invocation, continue to realize that you are in the presence of the
substance of pure Being and that you are immersed
in the light of Being, that this light from on high
saturates you from the crown of your head to the

soles of your feet. Then in order that you may receive an even greater outpouring of the Holy Spirit, repeat the Lord's Prayer as follows:

Our Father who art in heaven,
Hallowed be thy name.
Thy kingdom come.
Thy will be done
   In earth, as it is in heaven.
Give us this day our daily bread.
And forgive us our debts,
   As we also have forgiven our
    debtors.
And leave us not in temptation,
   But deliver us from evil.
For Thine is the kingdom,
     and the power, and the glory,
     for ever. Amen.

These words of Jesus' connect the soul directly with the celestial realm. With the Holy Spirit paramount in consciousness, the vision is quickened and you discern that you dwell consciously in your physical body, your soul body, and your spiritual body; that these three bodies must be merged in one in order to bring into manifestation that imperishable body which was demonstrated by Jesus Christ.

In conclusion, resolve that from this time on you are conscious of your I AM power and dominion, that henceforth you consciously direct your life in the light of Spirit, that your heart and your head are working together in all wisdom and power. You will perceive by this time that you are gaining a firmer grip on the power of the word in the palms of your hands and in the soles of your feet between the ball of the foot and the heel. This tends to place you on a firm foundation and to give you a greater consciousness of the unfolding processes going on during the rearing of the permanent dwelling place of Spirit.

We are indeed the masterpiece of Almightiness. With the throne of the Lord set up in our hearts, with the mantle of the Holy Spirit wrapped about us, and consciously working with the one creative power of the universe, we are free to build for ourselves not only perfect souls but also indestructible body temples.

Chapter 2

Faith

Affirmation: *Jesus Christ is now here raising me to His consciousness of unfailing faith, and I abide in Him.*

> Faith, mighty faith, the promise sees
> And rests on that alone;
> Laughs at impossibilities,
> And says it shall be done.
> —*Charles Wesley*

FAITH *is;* it is an attribute of God. Faith is purely spiritual; it knows nothing less than supreme assurance. Faith is dauntless; it knows no defeat. Faith is the quality of the mind that moves and molds ideas and brings them to concrete expression. Faith is the assurance or confidence of the mind that invisible substance is the source of visible material things. Modern science says that the cosmic ether is the mother of matter. Metaphysically we find that the cosmic ether is the light that the mind expresses when it holds to a definite idea. "By faith we understand that the world was created by the word of God, so that what is seen was made out of things which do not appear" (Heb. 11:3).

As rays of sunshine creep through tangled vines and shed their warmth and glow in the dark, damp

217

corners of the earth, so faith creeps through the dark, tangled meshes of human thought and radiates its strength, hope, and courage.

Faith enables us to see conditions as they are in the realm of reality. The basis of all Christian endeavor is faith. Without this vital factor Christianity is neither stable nor scientific. Faith enables us to see through the shadowy forms of false concepts—the creations of the natural man—and behold the real. Faith is the key that unlocks the door to the kingdom of the heavens; looking through the eyes of faith we behold people as the prism through which Divine Mind is endeavoring to flash into expression its perfect creation.

God lives in each heart, and those who consciously dwell in the secret of His presence come to understand the creative powers of the universe. Into this "secret place of the Most High" no thought of disease or destruction can enter. Here the healing, soothing balm of divine faith pours itself out, seeking to expand and to enlarge and make alive God's perfection in the whole consciousness. It even penetrates into the environment, bearing everywhere a sustaining trust that never wavers, never grows less, making the whole scheme of life one unbroken story of happiness, of joy, of love, and of abundance.

It is the constant mingling and intermingling of the conscious intelligence with faith that establishes the healing consciousness. This consciousness, built on the rock of faith, becomes more and more fearless and free, and finally comes forward and says,

"Behold, I am the Word made flesh. No task is too hard for me."

Our true ideas are always from God. The yearning desire of these divine ideas in the heart causes mind action, and through this movement the divine ideas are borne by faith into consciousness and produce thought. Thus the faith consciousness, once established, is constantly fed from the very fount of faith and grows stronger continually. God is the one source, and the knowledge that God is all and that all things not made by Him are unreal fills one who is working from principle with an immeasurable assurance. It gives us the firm conviction that all conditions of mind and body are ours to conquer through Christ.

Faith works on and on and on after all reason is exhausted. When set into activity according to law, faith will lay hold of the very basic substance of Being and create just what is needed to perfect the desired demonstration. Let us work to attain the faith vision that gives us the true prospectus of the realm of reality.

To illustrate how faith through Jesus Christ is called into spiritual action, picture a beautiful city, a city where there is no night. From the heart of the city flows a wonderful river whose water is clear as crystal; on the banks of the water is the tree of life, bearing twelve kinds of fruit every month. However, this beautiful city is encompassed by a high, thick, stone wall. There are no openings, and you are on the outside and wish to enter. The wall is so high that you cannot climb over it. The only way for you to gain entrance is to work your way through the rock. As you walk around the wall meditating upon the situation and wondering just how to begin, suddenly you come to a hole in the wall where another has made his way before you. Your way is made easy through the efforts of this pioneer, who has dared to cut a way through the thick, dense wall of materiality.

This picture illustrates the work that Jesus Christ has accomplished for you and for me in the development of faith in God. The beautiful city represents the potential kingdom of heaven within the soul; the river represents the river of life; and the twelve different kinds of fruit symbolize the fruit of Spirit, the twelve fundamental faculties represented in the life of Jesus by the Twelve Apostles.

Through faith in Jesus Christ we may enter into the spiritual kingdom and begin mentally to lay hold of our good. The one who has unfolded unwavering faith in God has unlimited power. Jesus was conscious of this wonderful power when He said, "Lazarus, come forth," even though Lazarus had lain in the tomb for four days. Jesus advised, recommended, even commanded that we unfold this wonderful faculty, an enduring power that never grows less. True faith can only be known to the practical Christian. In its spiritual reality it is beyond the comprehension of the artistry of poetical words. Spiritually, faith is a dynamic force that can only be described in scientific terms by seers and sages. It is one of the fundamental laws governing us and the universe, and it is directly related to the underlying substance of the universe. The definition of faith in Hebrews 11:1—"Faith is the assurance of things hoped for, the conviction of things not seen"— is a true statement.

Jesus said:

"Whatever you ask in prayer, you will receive, if you have faith" (Mt. 21:22).

"According to your faith be it done to you" (Mt. 9:29).

"Your faith has made you well" (Mk. 5:34).

"If you have faith as a grain of mustard seed, you will say to this mountain, 'Move from here to there,' and it will move; and nothing will be impossible to you" (Mt. 17:20).

These are all golden Truths given for our use.

At the center of the brain is the pineal gland. This gland is known to Truth students as the faith center, symbolized by Jesus' disciple Peter, and faith is the "rock" upon which He founded His church. When the inner eye is illumined with spiritual faith, a ray of light—the pure white, pearly light of Spirit—steady and unwavering, is often seen in the silence. So unfaltering and resolute is this ray of the spiritual light of faith that it seems as unmovable as a star in the heavens. However, it is only a symbol letting us know that the spiritual work has been done.

The exercises given herewith are for the purpose of illumining our consciousness until we realize that we have penetrated into the four-dimensional realm, the kingdom of the heavens that Jesus taught was within the soul.

For the beginning of this exercise repeat the whole of the "I AM" exercise given in Chapter 1. With the attention still at the great nerve center, take up next the thought of infinite faith. Affirm: *Through Jesus Christ the faith of almighty God is quickened within me.*

After you have gained a good realization of Omnipresence as faith, follow the radiance of Spirit that leads to the faith center, the pineal gland, at the middle of the head; then realize this same prayer: *Through Jesus Christ the faith of almighty God is quickened within me.*

Be perfectly relaxed and receptive to Spirit, and know that you are conscious of the spiritual power descending from the spiritual center, the crown of the head, showering you with new faith.

The tiny ray of pure light that is often discernible in the silence at the faith center is simply a result of the radiation or vibration of the word of faith upon which you are concentrating. When the power of the word reaches a certain degree of intensity, the light of faith becomes visible. Do not try to perceive this ray; by so doing you hinder your own unfoldment. Do the spiritual work quietly, remaining perfectly poised and relaxed. The Lord will take care of the results. Now (with you working with it) allow the Presence to drop slowly down to the love center just back of the heart, and declare: *Faith works through love.*

Then allow the Presence, the light of Spirit, to drop down into the soles of the feet, and repeat this declaration: *Understanding faith is now expressed through me.*

At the conclusion of the exercise, allow the Presence (while you continue to cooperate) to organize itself just back of the heart and stomach. Again realize: *Faith works through love.* During this realization *consciously know* that the windows of your soul are open toward the heavens of your mind, that the spiritual light as pure illumination is descending upon you, and that through faith you are steadily developing the Lord's body. End the exercise first with a realization of infinite love; then finish with the Lord's Prayer.

You will remember that the instructions in Chapter 1 are to keep the conscious mind, which operates through the front forehead, always fully aware of all that is taking place. Therefore, after you have finished, be sure that the conscious mind is awakening to the extent that it has perceived clearly every step of the way. At the close of the exercise, for the sake of balance, it is well to dwell consciously in the feet and even beneath the feet, also to throw the attention down into the palms of the hands, realizing that faith must always be accompanied with works, that nothing is yours unless you express it.

This being true, at the close of this exercise (also at the close of all the other exercises that follow), as you go forth to associate with others, know that your new realizations are freely finding expression in and through you, especially through the breast, the vital center of expression being at the point in the thorax, the lower part of the sternum, where the last of the true ribs is attached to the sternum. Also realize that your words are growing in power and intelligence and that you are strengthening a center of expression at that point where the upper lip is joined onto the base of the nose. By recognizing this, you will find that your voice will develop a richness and trueness that you as well as your friends will appreciate. Also know that a new light (illumination) is penetrating the seat of the conscious mind (front forehead) and that even your brow radiates the light of Spirit.

CHAPTER 3

⋙⋘

Strength

Affirmation: *Jesus Christ is now here raising me to His consciousness of sustaining strength, and I rest in joy and peace.*

THE REALIZATION of the Jesus Christ presence as sustaining strength is a stronghold in consciousness that fortifies us against all adverse conditions. Nothing so uplifts, nothing so frees from care and worry, nothing so brings the thought of victory as being established in that sustaining strength which cannot know weakness. To have the strength of character that makes life seem effortless, nonresistant, is to have the inward joy that no one can take away.

When Jesus withstood the temptations in the wilderness, He proved beyond all question that He possessed the strength of character that the Almighty required of Him. We are working for this same unfoldment. To be established in the consciousness of sustaining strength means that we have overcome as Jesus Christ overcame. The joy of the overcomer may be ours. When we hold our ground in the face of temptation and refuse to yield to the allurements of the world or of sense consciousness, no doubt the very angels shout for joy. True strength of character, though nonresistant, withstands the tricky, treacherous movements of the adversary in any guise; all shafts of error directed its way meet with defeat.

Among the apostles of Jesus Christ, Andrew symbolizes strength. The strength center is in the small of the back. Spiritual strength, the fruit of prayer and of meditating on strength, is born in the silence of the soul and reflected into the body at the strength center.

The eagle is the symbol of strength and victory. Solomon, meditating on the marvelous outworking of God's unbreakable laws, said that one of the things which was too wonderful for him was *the way of an eagle in the air.* The eagle is the expression of abounding strength. He mounts up into the air to an unbelievable height and from this altitude focuses his eye on the ground below and spots his prey. He rises above the cyclone; he outflies the wind. As is the way of an eagle in the air, so is the way of man when he fully realizes his divinity. Those who deem themselves to be finite, to be apart from the Infinite, cannot know of the possibilities of spiritual man, cannot dream of the possibilities of spiritual man.

All strength is from God. However, its manifestation is according to the mold of thought into which this precious essence is poured. Often we appropriate and try to use spiritual strength in worldly ways. This always leads to failure. In the seventeenth chapter of Ezekiel, Jehovah presents a riddle to the house of Israel. An eagle with great wings and long pinions, full of feathers, evidently from Babylon, comes unto Lebanon, takes away the top of a cedar, cuts off the topmost of the young twigs, and carries the cedar top to a land of traffic, to a city of merchants; he also takes good seed from the land and plants it in fruitful soil, beside many waters. The growth that springs from this planting is of low stature, the branches turn toward the eagle, and the roots are under him.

The solution of the riddle is that the eagle of Babylon that comes to Lebanon is an organized aggregation of strong, selfish, worldly thoughts, intent on trafficking in spiritual powers. The scheme proves a failure. Spiritual unfoldment is attained by each individual soul's establishing conscious at-one-ment with the Jehovah mind through Jesus Christ. Therefore, it cannot be bought or stolen; the unbreakable laws of the Infinite insure against all such attempts.

Truly to live the life of Spirit, one must be spiritually strong. One must withstand every test. Spirit's symbol of vigor, success, and victory is joy. We are joyous only when we are strong physically, mentally, and spiritually. Some persons are injured by having criticism, often of an unjust character, hurled at them. Their need is for the unfoldment of a strength of character that can handle prejudices and jealousies without resistance. If such souls are versed in metaphysical teachings, they know that Truth needs no defense; they know how to wrap themselves about in the protecting mantle of the Lord, how to rest quietly under the shadow of the Almighty during an onslaught, how to emerge strong and joyous after attack has spent its fury, and how to live life so that criticism may seem only a jest.

In Ecclesiastes, the twelfth chapter, a sorrowful picture is drawn of man so weakened by evil that life is a burden. His senses all buried in darkness, man is ready to welcome death; he is waiting for the *silver cord* to be loosed and the *golden bowl* to be broken so that he can hide himself in the grave.

The *silver cord* here referred to may be compared to the spinal cord that runs along the inner walls of the spinal column; the *golden bowl* is the abdominal wall that contains and supports the digestive organs. When the *silver cord* is loosed, and *the golden bowl* is broken, death results.

Death has no part in spiritual life. Our senses are keen and illumined. The ever-unfolding, ever-renewing Spirit of infinite strength sustains us, and we go from glory to glory. Realization of spiritual strength at the strength center, the small of the back, acts as an invigorating tonic to the *silver cord*. Spiritual strength flows freely along the nerves and penetrates into every cell and fiber of the *golden bowl*. The whole body temple is uplifted and vitalized.

For the exercise in the silence, first follow diligently the outline given in the first exercise in Chapter 1. Realize your I AM identity with Being. With your conscious mind realize that the light of

Spirit is descending from the spiritual center in the crown of the head. Then with the attention at the point designated as the great solar nerve center, back of the heart and stomach, repeat the invocation. Realize that you are in the presence of pure Being and immersed in its light. As you continue, you will come into the conscious knowledge that you are wrapped about in a mantle of light (pure understanding), that your feet are shod in sandals of light, and that every impulse of your soul is to express fully the Christ of God.

Next, for the special unfoldment of spiritual strength, you will continue to allow the Presence to dwell at the center of your being. Then affirm: *I am one with infinite strength.*

Next allow the Presence to drop to the small of the back and realize that the light of Spirit—which you feel but do not see—is descending from the crown of the head and organizing itself at the strength center. During this outpouring hold steadily to this thought: *I am one with infinite strength.*

You will feel new strength awakening within you. Next let the Presence ascend to the power center at the root of the tongue; then hold steadily to this thought: *I have power to express the sustaining strength of Spirit.*

Now allow the Presence to descend to the life center, the lowest part of the abdomen. There affirm: *The pure, undefiled life of Jesus Christ is expressed in and through me, and I am strengthened and sustained in all my ways.*

Next allow the Presence to return to the great center of being just back of the heart and stomach. There take up this word: *The joy of the Lord is a wellspring within me, and I am established in divine strength.*

Dwell consciously at that point, knowing that you are firmly established in the garden of spirituality within your own soul, that the light of Spirit is descending from the spiritual center, the crown of the head, and that new strength is flowing to every part of your being. The Truth is that the whole body temple is the garden of God and that every cell and fiber is made sweet and strong by this baptism of the Holy Spirit. You have a strong hold on the body temple when the I AM, the Christ, is established in your consciousness and is free to express itself from the very center of your being.

Close the exercise by repeating the Lord's Prayer.

It is well for the sake of balance, after you have finished the exercise, to throw the attention for a time into the palms of the hands and tips of the fingers, also into the feet, and then even beneath the feet, realizing that you are planted on the firm foundation rock of Truth.

CHAPTER 4

Wisdom

Affirmation: *Jesus Christ is now here raising me to His consciousness of divine judgment, and the wisdom of God is expressed in all that I think, say, and do.*

THE POWER by which we are justified or condemned is within us. Understanding this power, we see that the kingdom of the heavens is all about us, above us, beneath us, within us; that God is in His kingdom; and that every event of life is stamped with the judgment of God.

Logic and reason prove that every event of life bears the stamp of the judgment of the Almighty, regardless of what construction a judge of manmade law may place upon it. For a time this may seem untrue, but when the whole proposition has been thoroughly sifted, the conclusion will be found to bear the stamp of the judgment of God.

When a person is faced with stupendous issues, when he sees that only the wisdom and the judgment of God can save the day, he is likely to become very meek and lowly and to seek earnestly for the inner light.

When Solomon was a young man, he was selected king by his father David. Solomon's quick discernment revealed to him the whole situation just as it was. He was inexperienced and untried. His elder half brothers looked upon him as a hindrance to their progress. Any one of them would have relieved him of his kingdom had an opportunity to do so presented itself. Their personal interest was involved; therefore, they watched Solomon's every move, hoping he might make some mistake that they could use to rouse the people against him. But Solomon knew that the Lord, through David his father, had chosen him king. With this conviction in his mind he felt that he was on a firm foundation; he was not to be driven about by misgivings and fear. With deep concern but with peaceful heart, he turned to question the Helper within.

On one occasion, as he earnestly endeavored to make the inner union with that spiritual wisdom, which he instinctively felt was waiting to be called into activity, the calm assurance of Spirit ascended within his soul and he fell asleep. Then in a dream the Lord appeared to him and told him that he could have whatsoever he asked. Solomon said:

"And now, O Lord my God, thou hast made thy servant king in place of David my father, although I am but a little child; I know not how to go out or come in. And thy servant is in the midst of thy people which thou hast chosen, a great people, that cannot be numbered or counted for multitude. Give thy servant therefore an understanding mind to govern thy people, that I may discern between good and evil; for who is able to judge this thy great people?"

—1 Kings 3:7-9

In this prayer Solomon dedicated himself to the service of the Lord and laid upon the altar all his powers, all his possibilities, waiting for the judgment of God to be stamped upon him. Because of his unselfish choice, not only was his desire granted but riches and honor and long life were assured him by the Lord.

By reviewing Solomon's wonderful career as a ruler, we can better understand the breadth and depth and strength of the spiritual realization in this prayer, and know better to what degree he was able to let the spiritual powers work and act through him. In its original impetus every event of life is stamped with the judgment of God.

Solomon was made strong by test and trial. Each of our faculties is brought forth by use and by tests of our strength. As children of God we must master every mortal limitation. In order even to approach the divine throne, we must have power to judge aright every impulse that arises within the human heart, to judge aright the intense desire back of seeming appetite and passion, and our spiritual faculties must also be strengthened by use and tested by trials until we are accounted safe and sure by the great Judge of all.

So let us rid our minds of man-made standards of judgment and seek the inner wisdom that reveals that life is indeed a scientific proposition, the object of which is to bring forth the divine qualities of the superman.

One meaning of the word *Solomon* is "peace." It

is said that when this wise king was approaching even his most strenuous tests, he was the personification of peace. Perfect peace is always a forerunner of victory.

Every soul has free access to the source of wisdom within. As we approach the divine source of wisdom and begin to realize our oneness with it, we find that we are evolving a higher intelligence than that of the intellect and that we are learning the greatest of all sciences, the science of mind. We find that the primal principles of Being are pure ideas and that these ideas express themselves in pure words and thoughts. Divine wisdom, divine judgment, has in it the essence of goodness. When we really live in perfect relation to principle, we shall have the power to combine ideas rightly and so manifest wholeness and perfection in mind and body.

In all wisdom, we must consciously possess our bodies. In fact, we must not only consciously but also subconsciously possess our bodies. This ability is attained through the wise development of the twelve spiritual faculties.

For the exercise in the silence, first take up the exercise in Chapter 1, following step-by-step the outline given there, with the conscious mind in the front forehead fully aware of what is taking place. You will become more and more aware that the Christ of God is awakening within you, and that you are even consciously forming new perceptive faculties not only in the front forehead but throughout your whole being, putting on the Christ, and calling into manifestation the indestructible body temple.

After you have attained a satisfying realization of omnipresent God-Mind and become conscious of the outpouring of the Holy Spirit, continue allowing the divine presence to dwell at the point designated as the great solar nerve center; then take up the thought of infinite wisdom, spiritual judgment, and affirm: *Divine wisdom is awakened within me, and my soul rejoices.*

Then allow the Presence to go to the judgment or wisdom center, at the pit of the stomach, and affirm that the wisdom of Almighty God through Jesus Christ is descending upon you from the spiritual center, the crown of the head, and that you are appropriating and assimilating it in the spirit of love. Divine judgment is ever proclaiming that wisdom, symbolized by Jesus' disciple James, and love, symbolized by Jesus' disciple John, must work together. Affirm: *God is the name of the everywhere present wisdom in which I live, move, and have my being. Divine wisdom is awakened in me; I love to express divine judgment.*

Hold this statement until the whole being is illumined with spiritual light.

The great positive and the great negative at the center of our being are wisdom (judgment), at the pit of the stomach, and love, in the heart. In the development of the twelve powers, these faculties are paramount; they are closely related and work together in producing the strongest vibrations known to the body. Jesus called James and John "sons of thunder," a title symbolizing the powerful vibrations produced by these faculties. Wisdom is a great dynamic force that carries its power to the love center. In the action and reaction between these two centers we get our greatest realizations and most wonderful spiritual radiations. Wisdom and love, when combined, produce peace and poise, a great dynamic spiritual center symbolized by the city of Jerusalem.

Next allow the Presence, the light of Spirit, to return to the great solar nerve center back of the stomach and heart. Repeat this affirmation: *God has not given me the spirit of fear but of power, and of love, and of a sound mind.*

Then allow the Presence to enter the love center, the heart itself, and declare: *I love to express the wisdom of God. My heart beats in perfect accord with the great loving heart of God. I gladly put on the breastplate of peace, poise and power.*

Next allow the Presence to return to the great solar nerve center, and repeat the Lord's Prayer.

After you have finished this exercise it is often good to realize and affirm that your conscious mind is aware of the spiritual process going on. Then let the Presence drop down into the feet. Here realize that you are clothed in perfect understanding and peace.

As previously stated, these exercises are not to be pushed but used with discrimination.

CHAPTER 5

꧁꧂

Love

Affirmation: *Jesus Christ is now here raising me to His consciousness of infinite love, and my soul is filled and satisfied.*

J ESUS CHRIST was a carpenter. His mission on Earth was to construct a spiritual body temple, to unfold a spiritual soul, and to teach us the spiritual laws involved, in order that we might follow Him.

We are apprentices in Jesus Christ's workshop. Every day we are working to unfold soul qualities like those expressed by the Master—soul qualities that make us always lovable, strong, pure, and perfect. We know that the body is the fruit of the soul and that as we unfold spiritual qualities within the soul, the body goes through a process of refining, of upliftment. This process must continue until we demonstrate bodies fashioned after the pattern of His glorious body.

In this lesson we take up the thought of divine love. In the spiritual body the love center is the heart, symbolized by Jesus' disciple John. John loved the Master. During Jesus' journeys with His disciples through Palestine, John was almost continually by the Master's side. Even when Jesus was crucified and all the other disciples fled, John was not far from the Master. While John was in exile on the island of Patmos, he was *in the Spirit on the Lord's day* and was lifted up in consciousness until he beheld a vision of the perfect man, Jesus Christ in all His glory. Thus love beholds the transforming, uplifting power of the Christ.

Love holds soul and body together. Love is the attractive force that draws our good to us according to the depth and strength of our realization of love.

A number of years ago I went into the foothills of the Ozarks on a vacation. I stayed in a wonderful little home near a forest. The hearts of the people who dwelt in this home were filled with love for the birds, the squirrels, and all the other creatures of the forest. They called the creatures "the little people of the forest," and were continually trying to win their friendship. It was a source of pleasure to these people to give food and shelter to the little people of the forest—such action dissolves any tendency toward personal selfishness. They built birdhouses, and they put out food and water even in summertime. They won the confidence of a redbird. First, he flew down onto the porch and ate the crumbs placed there; then, he came to the open doorway for food; and finally, he came stepping into the kitchen. His visits were a joy to all the household.

I believe that in befriending the forest creatures these people were unfolding the faculty of unselfish love, which is of far more value in soul unfoldment than a course in the best college.

Just as these gentle people won the hearts of the forest birds, so God must win *our* hearts. But we must know what God *is* before we can love Him. The path that leads to true soul unfoldment leads to adoration of the great cause of all. We learn to adore God when we find that He is a God of love, willing to pour out His good upon us and to befriend us in every way. Just as the confidence of the wild creatures of the forest is won through love, so God through love is gently wooing us. God does not force or suppress the wild, uncultivated forces within the heart, but He gently opens avenues through which these forces may express themselves constructively.

Let us bless the parents of the present day who love their children wisely and who are not suppressing them or trying to force them into a certain mold, but are allowing them to be guided and directed by the indwelling Christ. Many persons today, as a result of being forced or suppressed in their youth, have hard, unyielding places in the subconscious mind that do not give up readily to the power of the word. Our hearts must be won for God. This winning is easy when we learn to know God as Spirit. All the wild, uncultivated forces in us must be won for God, but they must be won under the law of love. The rushing, jostling life of today often forgets love. Let us remember love. Let us endeavor always to cultivate this wonderful faculty. Just as John radiated love, so let us radiate it. Let us feel the warm love of Jesus Christ in our hearts. Let us realize love and send out thoughts of love until we are lifted above all thought of materiality.

In a magazine some years ago there was an article in which the author stated that the actors in the movies of that day often employed music to awaken their inner powers before appearing before the camera. Each had the music that he [or she] loved best: Thomas Meighan would have nothing but Irish jigs; Will Rogers listened to ukulele music; Pauline Frederick used but one tune, "Rockaby-Baby"; Irene Rich listened to Scotch ballads played on the violin. Often these persons had to wait for hours in their makeup before they were called on for their parts, but each one knew how to arouse his [or her] emotional nature by listening to the music that he or she loved best.

The music that *we* love best is the joyous, triumphant voice of the Christ singing through the inner recesses of our souls. The loving voice of the Christ awakens in us the spiritual powers that strengthen, uplift, and redeem.

For the exercise in the silence, first follow the outline given in Chapter 1. Repeating the Lord's Prayer, with the presence of the Holy Spirit at the great nerve center back of the heart and stomach, gives the indwelling Christ opportunity to command, through love, the twelve faculties, and to direct them in regenerative processes. Then continuing to dwell at the point designated, take up this thought: *I have faith in the supreme power of love.*

Love and wisdom always should go hand in hand.

Next allow the light of Spirit to descend into the heart and then to the pit of the stomach, at the wisdom center. At each point hold this thought: *Divine love and wisdom are united in me. I will sing of lovingkindness and of justice.*

Then allow the Presence to descend into the renunciation center, in the abdominal area. Here hold this thought: *The forgiving love of Jesus Christ cleanses, purifies, and redeems me.*

Then follow the Presence to the heart center and realize that the law of love is written in your heart. Try to imagine the deep, tender love of the Almighty that must have filled the heart of Jesus when He said, "I and the Father are one." Realize that in Spirit, soul, and body you are made perfect through the power of divine love.

But always bear in mind that love and wisdom must find expression through the conscious mind. With the I AM expressing itself at the point designated as the solar nerve center, and realizing that all the windows of your soul are open toward the spiritual center (the crown of the head), know that the conscious mind (front forehead) is aware of your new spiritual realization and is using it freely in contact with your world, that you are expressing the love of God in all your ways, and that your spiritual realizations shine out through your eyes and express themselves in your voice. Close the exercise with the Lord's Prayer, the attention being kept at the point designated as the great solar nerve center.

CHAPTER 6

Power

Affirmation: *Jesus Christ is now here raising me to His consciousness of divine power, and I am established in the mastery and dominion of Spirit.*

J
ESUS CHRIST promised that we shall receive power when the Holy Spirit comes upon us. The Holy Spirit is God in action. Since the activity of Spirit gives us power, we must logically conclude that power is a force generated from God through the activity of our words and thoughts. We receive added power when we set into action deeper realizations of the love, the wisdom, the strength, the life, and the zeal of the Almighty. Imagine if you can the powerful activity of these God attributes in all the disciples of Jesus, who were gathered in Jerusalem on the day of Pentecost, a few weeks after the Ascension.

"When the day of Pentecost had come, they were all together in one place. And suddenly a sound came from heaven like the rush of a mighty wind, and it filled all the house where they were sitting. And there appeared to them tongues as of fire, distributed and resting on each one of them. And they were all filled with the Holy Spirit and began to speak in other tongues, as the Spirit gave them utterance."

—Acts 2:2-4

242

The expression of power is regulated by our thoughts and our words. Jesus' apostle Philip symbolizes power. Power expresses itself through soul and body at the point in the throat where the hyoglossus muscle is located.

Christian metaphysicians call this place in the throat the power center. Power operates through the nerve aggregations in the throat that control the larynx. The larynx is symbolized in Scripture by Galilee. Also, the ductless gland known as the thyroid is directly connected with the power center.

The power center may be compared to the amplifying or stepping-up device of the radio. The audio amplifier in a receiving set simply increases the power of the voice of the singer or speaker until his words may be heard at great distances. In the human organism, the life current is harnessed by the power center, where it comes under the control of the I AM and is spoken into expression or is intelligently directed to its work in soul and body.

The thyroid gland placed across the front of the throat was the first of the ductless glands to yield its secret to science. By allowing the Presence, the light of Spirit descending from the spiritual center, the crown of the head, to organize itself at the thyroid gland (including the very base of the neck), and then realizing that the all-knowing power of the word of God is poured out from on high at these points, we allow the working intelligence of the word to be so greatly enhanced that the whole being becomes illumined; added power and control are felt throughout the whole body temple. However, such an exercise should not be of long duration, at least before one is well developed in the art of calling the disciples; and it should always be taken in connection with the thought of unselfish love. Otherwise, the personal ego tries to use the added power for its own glorification, which leads to defeat.

In Jesus' healing ministry He proved that there is a law back of and within all mind action and that intelligent cooperation with that law gives mastery and dominion. He knew this so well that His words brought forth instant results. He turned water into wine, He raised the dead and cast out demons. All those who seek spiritual healing and illumination need this dominion over life action. Since the power idea equalizes and controls the life energy in soul and body, we see that power is a branch of the tree of life.

There is no reason why we today should not receive such an outpouring of the Holy Spirit as was received by those gathered in Jerusalem on the day of Pentecost—if we have power to draw close enough to God in consciousness to receive the blessing. Consciously and subconsciously we are becoming aware that the activity of the Holy Spirit is governed by law and that this law exists in Being, that it is as exact and harmonious as the law that governs a musical production, and that it is as undeviating as the progressive steps one must take in solving a mathematical problem. God is the same yesterday, today, and forever. Jesus Christ's consciousness was an instrument through which God's laws operated during Jesus Christ's earthly ministry.

Our consciousness is the channel through which God's laws find expression; therefore, we can readily see that demonstration rests with us. We can become instruments through which the Holy Spirit expresses itself as it expressed itself through Jesus' apostles on the day of Pentecost.

Since we came to dwell on the Earth, we have worked continually for power, dominion, mastery; our influence is felt in all earthly conditions. The conclusion of those who have carefully studied the matter is that aeons ago the Earth was a wild and stormy place, a place of chaos, because it lacked the human controlling influence. When humans appeared, the turbulent conditions were gradually modified.

The unfolding of spiritual power reminds one of Benjamin Franklin's experiences with atmospheric electricity in what are known as his kite experiments. He believed that lightning would be a constructive power when controlled. He made a kite that would fly in rainy weather. As paper would not do, he made the kite of a silk handkerchief. He attached a bit of sharp-pointed wire to the head of the kite to serve as the upper terminus of what is now known as a lightning rod. To the lower end of the long kite string he tied a key. He knew that silk is a nonconductor of electricity; therefore, he tied a silk cord to the string by which to hold it. During a big electric storm Franklin sent his kite up among the clouds.

He stuck the key into a Leyden jar and waited. When he thought the key had had time to be charged with the electricity descending from the heavens along the kite string, he applied his knuckles to the key. There was a spark, really a little flash of lightning. The lightning was transmitted to the jar, and the jar was charged with electricity.

Moses on Mount Sinai exercised great spiritual power in his lofty realization of omnipotent wisdom when he received from Omnipresence the Ten Commandments and registered them on two tablets of stone. But Jesus Christ was the finished workman in the Lord's workshop. He could make perfect union with omnipresent energy and intelligence and thus receive great and glorious truths. His words were as lightning. He was illumined with light from on high. He said, "For as the lightning comes from the east and shines as far as the west, so will be the coming of the Son of man" (Mt. 24:27). Just as Benjamin Franklin harnessed the lightning, just as Moses used Omnipresence in receiving the Ten Commandments, so we through Jesus Christ use the attributes of God in our everyday lives.

Our aim in life should be to grow by unfolding the power of the living word. In order to do this, we must watch our words, and above all watch our thoughts. If we are careful to keep our thoughts right with God, we shall easily speak the right words. We should be truthful, for even little falsehoods hinder spiritual growth. On all occasions we must hew to the line, no matter where the chips fall.

We must also be careful that we do not do all the talking, but give God a chance to talk to us. *Be still, and know that I am God.*

For the exercise in the silence, first follow the outline given in Chapter 1. Get the realization of the outpicturing of the Holy Spirit throughout your whole being. Continuing to hold the attention at the great solar nerve center, affirm: *All power is given unto me in mind and in body.*

Then allow the Presence to ascend to the base of the neck, including the whole throat, and even the tip of the tongue. Realize that the light is pouring out upon you from the spiritual center in the crown of the head, and that you have the power to appropriate and assimilate this light. This is a good word to hold: *Thy name is Spirit. I know Thee as the one all-powerful, all-knowing Mind, now giving me full control of all the powers of Being.*

Then allowing the Presence, the Holy Spirit, to descend to the heart, meditate upon the power of divine love. Dedicate your realization of power to the loving service of the Lord. Holding the attention at the heart center, take up this prayer: *I am filled with power. The Christ of God expresses Himself in me and through me in love and power.*

Next allow the Presence to descend into the lowest part of the abdomen, the life center, with this thought: *The Jesus Christ purity is awakened within me. My "life is hid with Christ in God." The I AM power within raises up the natural man to the spiritual plane of consciousness.*

Again allow the Presence to ascend to the point named the great solar nerve center and affirm: *I am established in the peace, poise, power, and dominion of God. The Father in me is doing His work in love and in wisdom, and I rejoice in the fullness of my good.*

Close the drill by softly repeating the Lord's Prayer. During the whole drill be sure that the conscious mind in the front forehead is aware of the new power that you are generating. This tends to remold your perceptive powers more and more after the divine pattern. After the exercise sit for a few moments—first, with the attention in the palms of the hands and fingertips and then in the feet and beneath the feet.

May the word work mightily in you.

CHAPTER 7

Imagination

Affirmation: *Jesus Christ is now here raising me to His consciousness of divine imagination, and I see spiritual perfection everywhere.*

D IVINE IMAGINATION is the chisel we wield in molding the paradise of our inner-thought kingdoms. While in the silence, therefore, the thought forms we permit to be imaged in consciousness have as great an effect on our lives as our spiritual realizations. Intelligent seeing is a form of divine imagination; we should always behold ourselves in a state of keen, intelligent knowing. We should see God, good, as the foundation on which life is built; we should see God, good, as the source of life, and we should see ourselves majestically springing from that source.

It is through divine imagination that the soul first gets the impulse to expand. In the silence we learn to lift our vision above things as they commonly appear, and this helps to bring all the other faculties into captivity to the obedience of Christ. Thus we learn to acquaint ourselves with God and with God's world of reality. Divine imagination, working in consciousness, sees the kingdom of the heavens fashioned after the divine pattern shown on the mount of high spiritual illumination.

Under the old form of religion, imagination played an important part in picturing the result of sin, of missing the mark. Unsaved souls were supposed to be thrown into a boiling lake of brimstone, where they must burn forever. As we have evolved spiritually, we have come to understand the absurdity of such a thing. Spirituality is an unfoldment that the student acquires just as one develops one's musical talent. Patient practice brings forth the finished product. Just as an earthly father would not buy a piano and say to the child, "Now play, but if you make an error you are eternally damned," neither would the heavenly Father create a family and put them in a garden full of untried forces and say, "Now these powers are yours to use. Go ahead and use them, but if you make a mistake, you must suffer eternally for it."

Before the goal is reached, one perhaps must go through course after course of soul pruning; one must develop the power of specially "beholding" what is actually pure and true and perfect right in the face of that which only seems to be. Carlyle says that at the center of all life is music, and that he who sees deeply enough sees musically. By this same token, at the center of all life is the perfect pattern, the image and likeness of God, and he who sees spiritually sees through the eyes of God, beholds the good and the beautiful everywhere. To develop spiritually, we must unfold the spiritual vision.

Divine imagination exists, and it watches every

opportunity to express itself. No doubt you can re-call some memorable occasion when a noble, un-selfish impulse sprang up from within your soul, and before you knew it, you were acting upon that impulse. You know now that your divine nature, suddenly aroused, brought that unselfish impulse into expression. Your friends may have told you that under the sway of that impulse the whole expression of your face changed—the light in your eyes deep-ened, you were possessed of a new and wonderful strength of character. On this memorable occasion, your eyes saw what your soul had the ability to image and to hold. The eye of your mind saw the su-perb thing you were capable of bringing forth. In other words, you opened that inner door so that you could at least glimpse the kingdom of the heavens within. Such experiences make the soul hunger to live up to these noble impulses, to express the real Self. In other words, there is a constant soul craving to be fed on unselfish ideas.

Imagination is an attribute of God. It is the for-mative power of thought, the molding power of the mind. It is that which gives shape, tone, color to thinking. In Truth every word, every combination of words, has back of it an image, a thought picture. These images, these combinations of shapes working in omnipresent substance, mold our lives.

We all have free access to God; therefore, we have free access to divine imagination. Would you be strong, healthy, wise, lovable? Image yourself; think of yourself as strong, healthy, wise, lovable. Watch the deep, inner thoughts of your mind; back of them are images that are molding your life. Jesus Christ knew how the law of divine imagination works, and He molded His life after the divine pattern. That fact was what He had in mind when He said: "He who has seen me has seen the Father" (Jn. 14:9). He knew that He was the image of the Father brought into manifestation.

We find in reading the Bible that the prophets of old were well versed in the use of the imagination. They were guided by their visions and their dreams. There is a scientific law back of our visions of the night. Everything that happens in the outer world first takes place in the inner realm of thought. The inner realm of thought is where the Spirit of Truth operates, and when something that is vital in a person's life is about to take place, the Spirit of Truth makes it known to him in the manner that can best reach his consciousness. Often when one becomes still, as in sleep, the Spirit of Truth throws the message on the screen of the mind in thought pictures and the recipient calls it a dream. Of course, one must learn to read the symbols. If the message is good, all is well. If not, one should go into the silence and hold realizations for light, wisdom, and the transforming power of Spirit until the error is dissolved. Emerson said that nothing is so hideous or so unclean but that intense light will make it beautiful. This rule holds good in dissolving error-thought forces that are trying to manifest their power in one's life.

On the other hand we find that before Jesus Christ can be imaged in a dream, we must use those deep, powerful spiritual laws which bring forth the divine image. The same scientific law that governs dreams governs visions.

Just as the prophets of old were guided through the faculty of imagination, so spiritually quickened souls all down the ages have been guided by this same power.

Divine imagination, an instrument in the hands of the Spirit of Truth, often takes a prophetic turn; it has the power to read out of the law and let one know possibilities as they really are—what will take place if such and such thought forces continue to operate.

During the Revolutionary War, George Washington's strong right arm and active imagination were directive powers through which the Lord worked in laying the foundation stones of the United States of America. It is said that during the discouraging days of 1777, when Washington was encamped with his army at Valley Forge, a vision came to him. While he was on his knees praying, asking to be shown the right thing to do, a light shone round about him and a vision of a broad and prosperous country spread out before him. He recognized it as the future United States. In Truth he had made the contact with spiritual forces outpicturing what would inevitably come to pass. Washington's heart thrilled with exultation. The remembrance of that vision spurred him on to victory. After the colonists had won the war, that vision made him a tireless worker in helping to perfect the Constitution and to establish the country on a sound basis.

In the unfoldment of the other eleven faculties it is the activity of the imagination that causes the different colors to appear. For example, when in the silence the radiation of the word of power has reached a certain degree of intensity, the imaging faculty not only stamps the realization with shape or form, corresponding with the true worth of the realization, but it also causes the color blue-purple to appear. When the realization for love is held, the imaging power causes the color rose to appear, and so on.

The imaging power of the mind is symbolized by all the colors of the rainbow. However, when all these colors are brought to a focal point, a flow of white light is the result. Take this same billowy flow of light and pass it through a crystal prism, and it will come out on the other side of the prism broken up into its component parts, purple, green, pink, yellow, and so forth.

Jesus' apostle Bartholomew symbolizes the faculty of divine imagination. Between the eyes is a ganglionic nerve center, which when spiritually quickened will set into operation the divine imaging power.

For the work in the silence first take up the exercise given in Chapter 1, realizing that you are "in the presence of pure Being" and that you are "immersed in the Holy Spirit of life, love, and wisdom." Endeavor to see with the inner eye the real man, the real woman, within. Allowing the Presence to dwell at a point back of the heart, realize this prayer: *The image of the Christ is implanted within me.*

Realize that the quickening power of the word is bringing that divine image into manifestation. Then allow the Presence, the light of Spirit, to ascend into the seat of the imaging faculty, between the eyes, realizing this word: *I am the image and likeness of God in manifestation.*

Allowing the Presence to drop down to the heart center, affirm: *My heart is beating in perfect accord with the great heart of God. Through the eyes of love I behold everybody and everything pure and perfect.*

Next allow the Presence to drop down into the feet. Then affirm: *I am able to stand up straight before the Lord; I am walking perfectly before Him.* Then quietly let the Presence take up its abode back of the heart. Hold this prayer: *I am created in the image of God. I am created after the likeness of God.*

Then close the exercise with the Lord's Prayer. In conclusion, as in the previous exercises, drop the attention down into the feet, and let it dwell there for a while. By this time you will have discovered that by so doing you set into activity all the spiritual powers of your being.

CHAPTER 8

Understanding

Affirmation: *Jesus Christ is now here raising me to His consciousness of divine understanding, and all my mental activities are spiritual.*

FOR AGES the soul, confined in the prison of sense consciousness, has intensely desired a higher and better life than that which is compassed by the five senses. The struggling soul has craved an understanding heart, has prayed above all things to be led out of the darkness and the wilderness of the five-sense life into a new life, into something worthwhile. For ages, the only answer to this craving has been the hope of heaven after death, with the proviso that we accept the worm-of-the-dust theory and bow to pain and suffering as conditions placed upon us by God.

By meditation and by the innate logic of mind, which is really a process of cleaning the windows of mind so that we continually see a little more clearly, we have become conscious of our unity with the great source of almightiness, and have learned that through this unity we may be led into the light here and now. In other words, divine understanding is today awaking in our hearts.

For one to incline the ear to wisdom is to bend one's mind toward the universal mind of wisdom until one sets one's thoughts into action in a manner that will enable them to move in unison with Divine Mind. Just as the sunflower always keeps its face turned toward the sun, just as the trailing vine runs toward the light, so the inner forces of the soul must be turned toward the divine. To apply the heart to understanding means to work diligently and earnestly for the purpose of gaining a knowledge of the laws that govern life, and to strive to operate those laws.

Divine understanding is the perceiving power of the mind. Divine understanding is the eyes of its twin faculty, divine will. Divine will is the governing, directing power of the mind. These spiritual faculties operate through the front brain and are represented by the apostles Thomas (understanding) and Matthew (will). These powers working together have the ability to perceive in the invisible realm of thought, and to direct and bring the inner light from the unmanifest to the manifest world. They connect the inner world of thought with the outer world of manifestation.

In the beginning of spiritual unfoldment, divine understanding may seem to be operating in a dim light, to be clouded, indistinct, indecisive. But within each of us is a spiritual law of light (understanding) that, if we industriously affirm it, will develop in us the power to use the attributes of God and to understand their place and their work in the Deity. Spiritual understanding enables the consciousness to see and to feel spiritually. Spiritual understanding gives clear insight into everything; it remolds the mentality, and inspires the will to direct, to act, and to control.

At the beginning of a new year we often make resolutions, but we do not always live up to them. What is the stumbling block? We have been sincere in making the resolutions, but the old mental conceptions formed by limited understanding resist the new understanding, the new inspiration; they try to hold their ground. This resistance causes a letting down in consciousness. It takes patience, perseverance, industry to remold the perceptive and directive powers of the mind. But while the process may be slow, it is sure if we keep on. Our problem is to gather enough energy, power, love, wisdom, and pure light within to enable us to breathe divine liberation into the soul, into the very flesh—to arouse sufficient power to lift up the whole consciousness until we see with an understanding heart.

In these days we hear much about the garden of God; it is a theme for songwriters and for poets. The song "In the Garden" reminds us that Jesus walks with us and talks with us and tells us we are His own. What is this wonderful garden of God where the Christ dwells? Is it a place in the outer world? Have we ever analyzed it scientifically? Do we know just where this garden is? John, Jesus' beloved apostle, tells of his wonderful vision of the resurrected Jesus in the garden of God in Revelation 22:1-2:

"Then he showed me the river of the water of life, bright as crystal, flowing from the throne of God and of the Lamb through the middle of the street of the city; also, on either side of the river, the tree of life with its twelve kinds of fruit, yielding its fruit each month; and the leaves of the tree were for the healing of the nations."

This wonderful garden of God must be the whole body temple, and all the glorious things that John saw there must have been the outpicturing of his spiritualized soul thoughts, for the soul occupies the body temple, and its emanation is called the aura. Jesus symbolized the indwelling Christ in action. This river of living water is produced by the flow of spiritual thoughts through the soul. The ebb and the flow of spiritual thinking produce a fine essence of life, which flows through the nerves. This essence of life also courses through the blood. The river flowed *out from the throne of God and of the Lamb.* All things come from the word, and the throne denotes the establishment of the spiritual word within the soul, through which authority is given us to exercise power and dominion. *The tree of life with its twelve kinds of fruit . . . and the leaves of the tree were for the healing of the nations.* The picture given in this passage represents the soul's energy and life in the nervous system. There are two great branches to this tree of life: the sympathetic nervous system and the cerebrospinal nervous system. The great ganglia of the sympathetic system regulate the functions of respiration, circulation, and digestion, the nerve centers near the heart and the stomach being the central stations. This nervous system makes us feel joy or sadness, health or illness. The cerebrospinal system consists of the brain and the spinal cord, with branches to various parts of the body; it gives us the power to move.

This wonderful tree of life brings forth much fruit, symbolizing the unlimited power of Spirit to increase.

For a regenerative exercise in the silence, first take up the one given in Chapter 1. Then, still allowing the Presence to dwell at the point designated as the solar nerve center, declare that your body temple is the garden of God, that Jesus (the indwelling Christ in action) is standing in the midst directing and controlling the ebb and flow of your spiritual energies. Hold this thought: *The Christ of God is active in me; the breath of the Almighty gives me understanding. I am transformed by the renewing of my mind.*

Next, allowing the Presence to ascend to the front brain, to the understanding and the will center, meditate upon this thought: *Divine understanding is awakened in me, and I am divinely guided in all that I do. I see spiritually, I feel spiritually, I know spiritually.*

Then allow the Presence to drop down into the feet, holding this prayer: *My feet are placed on the firm rock of divine understanding. I am shod in sandals of pure gold. I am governed, guided, and directed by the wisdom and the power of the indwelling Christ.*

While the will and understanding faculties in the front forehead contact the mind, the feet represent the understanding and guiding power that contacts materiality.

Next, allow the Presence to rise to the point designated as the great solar nerve center back of the heart and stomach, and feel the spiritual flow from head to foot; realize again that your whole body temple is the garden of God, and that every spiritual center in this garden is imbued with the perfect understanding of Jesus Christ. Close the drill by softly repeating the Lord's Prayer. The Christ of God in the midst of you is mighty to heal, to guide, and to uplift. By this time you will have discovered that the unfoldment of the spiritual faculties is one of the most advanced of metaphysical developments and cannot be pushed. However, when one has learned how to harness and use these powers, one would not go back to the old methods any more than one who has learned the advantage of harnessing and using electricity would go back to coal oil and the old ways of living. A student who is working earnestly along the line of faculty unfoldment may become aware of growing pains. If the growing pains are too severe, it is sometimes best to cease the exercises in the silence for a period of time. After the student has thoroughly digested the inspiration already received and realizes that he is well poised and centered in the new light, the development may be continued.

CHAPTER 9

Will

Affirmation: *Jesus Christ is now here raising me to His consciousness of divine will, and I continually will to do His will.*

We will obey the voice of the Lord our God . . . that it may be well with us" (Jer. 42:6). Every great character of the Bible became great by learning to hear and to obey in all things the voice of the indwelling Christ. Moses' life reveals how nonresistance and obedience may lead one through the dangers of sense consciousness (Egypt) into light and freedom (the Promised Land). When Moses was born, his life was, from the viewpoint of man, in immediate danger. The king of Egypt had issued an edict that every male child born to the Israelites should be killed. This decree doomed Moses. But the spiritual nature wrapped in the soul of the young babe delivered him from the man-made law and brought him safely through every peril.

The great mother love in the heart of the woman who bore Moses caused her to hide him away during the first few months of his life. When she could no longer keep him in concealment, she made a basket of rushes, placed him in it, and set the basket among the reeds on the shore of the river Nile, with the prayer that God would bring the precious cargo into the hands of someone who could and would protect and save her child. God's hand protected the boat. An Egyptian princess, accompanied by her ladies in waiting, came to bathe in the Nile. She found the babe in his boat and adopted him. Thus, through God's guidance this little boy was placed where he received the best of care, where eventually every advantage of the land of Egypt was opened to him.

Moses became a great leader, a great lawgiver. The name *Moses* means "drawing out." Through the power of divine guidance he finally led the Children of Israel out of their Egyptian bondage and placed them on the path that led to the Promised Land.

The history of Moses is the history of every great character. Obedience to the guiding power of the indwelling Lord was the one thing that elevated him above the race.

We have gradually drifted away from our central I AM into the outer realms of consciousness, until today we dwell largely in the night of our minds; we have become involved in external entanglements and confusion until our consciousness has lost the real power of Spirit. We have become willful, which is the cause of much of our suffering. We have lost almost all conception of what it is to hear and to heed the voice of the indwelling Lord. We look to man-made laws and to man's opinions as standards of living and think that in worldly affairs there is no place for religion. The affairs of the world have been carried on independent of the higher powers, until today our civilization is approaching chaos.

But the awakening Christian of the present time is working early and late to learn of the quickening power of Spirit and is continually saying with Paul: "Let every person be subject to the governing authorities. For there is no authority except from God, and those that exist have been instituted by God" (Rom. 13:1). Mankind quickened by Spirit realizes that God is the one and only power, and it desires above all else to be guided and directed by that power. The devout soul is willing that the will of God shall be done, but may be uncertain as to the way. A good prayer for guidance is this: *I am guided, governed, and directed by the wisdom and the power of my indwelling Lord, and all my ways are ways of pleasantness, and all my paths are peace.*

We must do more than merely repeat this prayer; we must realize it in the very depths of our hearts until our every faculty and our every cell responds.

This realization opens the way so that the light of Spirit may descend from the higher realms of the mind and establish itself within the soul. How eagerly the awakening student seeks this newborn light. How eagerly he follows it, more than willing to prostrate himself before the throne of God, if by so doing he may be led out of the darkness of mortal ignorance into a better understanding of life. Thus, the quickened soul is learning to obey; the faculty of divine will that operates between absolute Truth and relative conditions is coming again, little by little, into activity in all our affairs.

Divine will is the mediator between God and us. It operates between the inner realms of mind and the outer manifestation. Among the apostles of Jesus Christ, Matthew symbolizes the will, the executive power of the mind. (He was a tax collector, who sat at the gate and exacted tribute from those who passed through.) Divine will (Matthew), together with its twin faculty, divine understanding (Thomas), operates in the forehead, the front brain. Every high spiritual realization—be it a realization of love, of power, or what not—should be gently brought to the attention of these twin faculties, the will and the understanding, because they make connection between the invisible world of thought and the outer world of manifestation.

Divine will is good will. In real spiritual unfoldment, when we become obedient to the indwelling Christ, will and understanding inquire into the real value of every thought that knocks at the door of consciousness; they learn its real value, and they make it pay tribute according to its worth.

Emerson said that one man was true to what is in you and me. That one man was Jesus Christ. Let us be true to ourselves. Let us be true to what is in us. I believe that obedience to the best that we know is the key that will unlock every door that opens into the spiritual realms. Let us be obedient. Each of us can be conscious of this inner guidance. By being meek and lowly, subservient to Spirit, we open the way for God's great loving will to enwrap us, to protect us, to lead us into the paths of peace, health, happiness, and prosperity, just as it protected Moses' little reed boat in the river Nile.

A good exercise for the silence is to go within and take up the exercise given in Chapter 1. Then, allowing the Presence to continue to dwell back of the heart and stomach, at the point designated as the great solar nerve center, realize that God and God's laws are all.

Then allow the Presence to ascend to the front forehead (the center of the twin faculties, will and understanding), and affirm: *The will of God is ever uppermost in my consciousness, and I am glorified in my understanding.*

Next, allow the Presence to drop down into the order center, back of the navel, and affirm: *My understanding is opened and my will is alert in the execution of the law.*

Gradually you will come to know that God's loving, sheltering will is within you and about you, and this realization will give you a consciousness of security and understanding. Then again allow the Presence to ascend to the point designated as the great central sun, and close the exercise by softly repeating the Lord's Prayer.

In conclusion, for the sake of perfect balance, throw the attention down into the feet and know that the will of God, working in the perfect understanding of the law, is having its perfect way in you. The feet represent that part of the body which contacts the earth, also the affairs of the world. Hence the great necessity of always preserving the consciousness of equilibrium and poise.

⟨⟨✦⟩⟩

CHAPTER 10

Order

Affirmation: *Jesus Christ is now here raising me to His consciousness of divine order, and I realize that the law of God is fulfilled in me.*

HAVING GONE to a theater to witness some wonderful play, how many of you for a while did little but observe the workings of the machinery auxiliary to the play? At exactly the right time the curtain went up. At a glance you were able to note the harmonious arrangement of the stage. The scenery and the furnishings were a suitable background for the scene that was to be enacted. The different characters were introduced at the right time, in just the order that would make the play most effective. Everything happened at the psychological moment. Order and system were so apparent that you could not help noticing them.

The same law of order and system that is necessary to a play is necessary to right relations among all the people. Were it not for the law of divine order, confusion would be apparent everywhere. Law and order are back of all manifestation. All creation is working through an evolutionary process under law. Especially is this true of humans in whom and through whom God carries forth creative law.

The perfect person is created as a perfect idea, which is to be manifested under the law of divine order. This perfect pattern (Christ) is working itself out through the flesh, coming into perfect manifestation under law and order.

We have free will, and in ignorance we often act in direct opposition to the divine law, but when we reach a certain stage of understanding, we strive earnestly to keep the divine law. We know that our freedom will come by cooperating intelligently with the law.

In working out our problems of everyday life, we should first take into consideration the relation that the problem bears to God, then to our fellowmen and ourselves. Next, we should lay hold of the ideas that are to be worked upon by divine law. As these fundamental ideas are incorporated into consciousness, they make contact with thought forces on various planes of action, and the many complex problems that arise in the course of the soul's evolution are harmonized under the higher law.

It is very clear that the safety of the people of the earth lies in the operation of the law of order upon which the universe is founded. To be happy we must act in accordance with God's eternal laws and allow them to work peacefully and thoroughly in and through all that we do. Divine law is not hard and binding; it expresses itself in freedom and joy.

Our so-called laws of civilization are in a way copied after the divine law, but personality has entered in, and thoughts of ambition, selfishness, and greed are dominant; therefore, man-made laws are colored with personal ambitions. To be overtaken by the law means, to one immersed in sense, to be convicted of crime and to be fined or imprisoned. One overtaken by the divine law—that is, one who has not acted in harmony with the divine law—suffers mental and physical imprisonment; he fails to grow spiritually and the reaction of the forces of life within him destroys his body. The illumined individual prays for greater strength, greater power to live in harmony with the law, counting it a privilege to pay the last farthing of the penalty that has been imposed because of his transgression of the law, for by so doing he enters to a greater degree into the heavenly kingdom.

The divine law of order working in the subconsciousness unearths buried talents, reveals hidden powers, and paves the way for their expression. The divine law of order coordinates the mind powers so that new inspirations may come forth and find unhindered recognition and lodgment in the conscious mind. The divine law of order emphasizes our overcoming power, thereby abolishing fear and despair. Sickness and weakness are never to be recognized as having a place in divine law and order. Health and freedom are always the outworkings of God's wondrous plan. In short, while we apparently are undergoing continual change, both physically and mentally, the changeless law of order is operating in the spiritual depths of being.

Our spiritual realizations blend in the subconsciousness and work to eliminate the weak and the negative; a wonderful law of order is at work there. There is a yoking and a pulling together of the spiritual powers to the end that both soul and body may be lifted up to the divine standard.

By broadly watching the results of the operation of the universal law, we perceive that the whole world is a stage and that each one has his part to play; we see that in us there is a specific spiritual faculty that, when unfolded, moves the machinery of mind, body, and affairs more perfectly, scientifically, harmoniously, and skillfully than the efficient stage manager handles a play.

In the development of the type man Jesus, James (son of Alphaeus) represents order. His work was to cooperate with the other disciples, just as the orderly movement of a play depends upon the cooperation of the players. The center of order in the body is located at a nerve center back of the navel. By employing prayer and meditation one may quicken the ganglionic nerve cells at the order center. It is through the navel that the unborn babe receives its sustenance from the mother; so it is through this order center that the soul, spiritually quickened, receives the divine manna direct from the Father-Mother God. Through our meditation and consecration, the spiritual laws are unfolded to us from within. Then our realization of God as the great Father-Mother is quickened, and not only do we discern the soul experiences that have been ours in

former lives, but it is revealed to us that certain un-
fulfilled desires have determined our present parent-
age. The inner realization corresponds with the outer
manifestation.

Divine order radiates its mighty power into the
other faculties and sets them into sustained activity
to the end that perfection shall be brought forth.
Thus, through the operation of divine order, the
greatness of the soul is demonstrated and the nature
of God is revealed.

For the regenerative exercise in the silence, first
take up the exercise given in Chapter 1. Continuing
to allow the Presence, the light of Spirit, to dwell at
the point designated as the great central sun, back
of the heart and stomach, affirm: *Divine order is
active in my mind, body, and affairs, and all things are
working together for my good.*

Realize that, under divine law, the rule of infinite Mind is awakened in you, and every function
and organ of your being is inspired with health,
harmony, peace, joy, and satisfaction.

Then let the Presence descend to the order center back of the navel, and affirm: *The law of the
Spirit of life in Christ Jesus has made me free from the law
of sin and death.*

As you dwell upon this powerful statement, realize that the light of Spirit from on high, from the
spiritual center in the crown of the head, is descending upon you, and that you are laying hold of
a new understanding of the divine law of life. Next
allow the Presence to center in the small of the

back, the strength center. Then, perfectly relaxed in mind and in body, affirm: *The law of divine order and harmony is satisfied in me, and I behold myself a tower of spiritual strength and stability.*

Then let the Presence ascend to the power center at the root of the tongue and base of the neck, and realize: *I am the power that sets into activity God's perfect law; every function of my mind, every organ of my body, is working to glorify the Father.*

Next, let the light of Spirit return to the order center just back of the navel, and declare: *Praise God, the law of divine order is satisfied in me, and I am at peace with all mankind.*

Then allow the Presence to return to the point designated as the great central sun; there realize that the laws of God are written in your heart and that your delight is to direct your life according to His laws. Close the exercise by softly repeating the Lord's Prayer.

After the drill is ended, throw the attention down into the feet and declare that your house is in order and that all the forces of your being are working to glorify God.

CHAPTER 11

───

Zeal

Affirmation: *Jesus Christ is now here raising me to His consciousness of divine zeal, and I enthusiastically express the inner spiritual urge.*

THERE IS A LAW not learned from books, but a knowledge of which is innate in every soul, that when consciously recognized and set into action makes the soul thirst to express itself in its fullness, even though at the same time the inrush of the Spirit may make one tremble from head to feet.

This is the law that upheld Jesus so wonderfully, so dauntlessly, when He stood before the high priest at His trial just before the Crucifixion, when the high priest questioned Him concerning His teachings, and He answered, "I have spoken openly to the world; I have always taught in synagogues and in the temple . . . I have said nothing secretly" (Jn. 18:20).

This law taught by Jesus is the law of divine enthusiasm—dauntless, unconquerable. It is the law that brings into expression the wonderful quality that we know as spiritual zeal.

The law of divine enthusiasm, spiritual zeal, is one of the most powerful laws operative in the king-

273

dom of the heavens. To speak always fearlessly, truthfully, and courageously makes for enthusiasm and establishes a confidence, a sureness that even the angels of heaven must notice and honor.

The world has been zealous in advocating reforms. The trouble with all reforms has been that those who were behind them have tried to compel others to change their ways without changing their hearts. When the principles of practical Christianity get a deep hold on one's consciousness, one is not only willing to change but to work continuously to lay hold of the spiritual powers that will transform him. Application of the fundamental principles of Christianity, that is, of love toward God and humanity, makes new creatures of men and women. This is true today, as it has been true all down the ages. But no great inspiration is going to emanate from a lukewarm religion; one must be zealous in one's work. Courageous, zealous religion is the power that transforms one, that makes one want to be on the right side of every proposition.

We hear it said very often that there is no place in the commercial world for religion, that religion is a thing to be used on the Sabbath, but that it is not practical for everyday affairs. There are many clear-thinking people who turn away from the church, presumably because it is of no value in their lives. Ministers are often troubled because they cannot make some people keenly interested in religion. The work of every minister is to put religion into the hearts of men and women and to keep religion uppermost in their thoughts. One cannot accomplish such work by picturing the negative side of life—by preaching that we are poor, miserable worms of the dust and that to be righteous we must be poverty-stricken. But we can accomplish that end by accepting and practicing the real principles of Christianity—which are practical, scientific, and substantial—and with the right mental attitude we will solve all the problems of the world. When a minister preaches the real religion, he is going to have his church filled with sound people who will be zealous to lay hold of and apply the Christ principles.

The successful businessperson learns that real success comes through service. God is the great servitor. We are successful to the degree that we truly serve; therefore, every zealous student should carefully study his own consciousness, should thoroughly study his own heart in order to see whether his zeal springs from the spiritual consciousness or from the personal consciousness. If his incentive is from the spiritual consciousness, if he is working to serve, then zeal broadens his vision, makes him alert, and adds sweetness and strength to his whole being. But if the impulse derives from his personal consciousness, his zeal merely adds impetus to his endeavors to gain personal ends, to further his own interests, even at the expense of other people. Selfish zeal will eventually eat up our life and substance, and leave us with starved, hungering souls, and with strained, hollow-eyed countenances. *For the zeal of thy house hath eaten me up.* Emerson pictures a person intoxicated with personal zeal as *inwardly drunk with a certain belief.*

Courage is a very vital part of religion. The courageous spirit is zealous to prove the strength and power of God. The courageous spirit glorifies God among the daily duties and trials of the world. Some levelheaded businesspeople know that it takes a courageous, zealous spirit to win out. They have not learned this in the church, but by experience; they have not yet come to know that religion, practical Christianity, gives these qualities. They have not discerned God as their business partner; they have not yet become aware that the something within them that leads them to success is the living Christ within their hearts. When they recognize this connection they will be zealous to know the deep things of religion, because they cannot afford to be without religion, scientifically understood and applied.

Spiritual zeal is one of the twelve fundamental powers of being, and is symbolized by Jesus' apostle Simon, the Cananaean. In the body its center of action is in the *medulla* at the base of the brain. By centering the attention at the base of the brain and realizing the quickening power of the Logos or Word, one causes new zeal and new courage to find expression in one's soul.

Zeal is the power that incites the other faculties to greater and ever greater activity. Zeal, courage, and earnestness give luster and color to the soul, just as the sparkle of the diamond gives it beauty.

When a person is truly working in the consciousness of spiritual zeal, he is zealous to express the spirit, zealous to serve God, to serve God's children; every impulse of his soul is to transmute low, selfish desires into those which conform to a high spiritual standard. Such a worker is a pearl of great price in the sight of God; his power is felt the world round.

Although some are overzealous for personal achievement, the mass of humanity has been listless, inactive, prone to wait for some outer power to stir it into action. Some have not realized their deep, spiritually zealous natures. Let us get beneath such listless inactivity; let us stir up the gift of divine courage within us, and we shall find new inspiration, new ideas waiting to be born into the world. Just as God is from everlasting to everlasting, so the courageous spirit of the Lord in our consciousness is eternal when once fully established.

For the regenerative exercise in the silence, first take up the one given in Chapter 1. Continuing to allow the Presence to remain at that point designated as the great solar nerve center, meditate upon the thought: *I am established in spiritual consciousness, and I am zealous to serve God, to serve humanity.*

Next let the Presence ascend to the base of the brain, the zeal center, and hold the prayer: *I am one with the ever-unfolding, ever-increasing Spirit of infinite courage, enthusiasm, and zeal.*

Then let the Presence descend to the wisdom center, and meditate upon the prayer: *Thou, O God, art always with me as indwelling infinite wisdom and spiritual judgment. I am zealous to know and to do Thy perfect will.*

Now allow the Presence to ascend to the faith center, the pineal gland, at the center of the head. At this point gently affirm: *Through faith I see into the kingdom of the heavens, and through spiritual enthusiasm I work to bring that perfect kingdom into manifestation.*

Now let the Presence return to the zeal center at the base of the brain. Resting at this point for a moment, affirm: *The quickening, vitalizing, free-flowing enthusiasm of Spirit is working in me mightily, transforming me into newness of life.*

Then let the Presence, the light of Spirit, drop down to the point back of the heart and stomach designated as the great solar center. Here gently affirm that you are zealous only to do the will of the Father. Close by quietly repeating the Lord's Prayer.

As in the previous drills be sure at the close that the conscious mind in the front forehead is aware of the whole procedure. Then drop the attention down into the feet and beneath the feet, and realize perfect balance and poise.

CHAPTER 12

Renunciation

Affirmation: *Jesus Christ is now here raising me to His consciousness of self-denial, and I realize that the cleansing, purifying power of the Holy Spirit is active in me.*

When humanity began to multiply on the face of the Earth and to express fleshly freedom, "the Lord saw that the wickedness of man was great in the earth, and that every imagination of the thoughts of his heart was only evil continually" (Gen. 6:5). Much grieved, the Lord said, "I will blot out man whom I have created from the face of the ground" (Gen. 6:7).

But there was one righteous man on the Earth, a man who even in the midst of wickedness walked with God continually. The Lord made known to this righteous man, Noah, the coming of a great deluge that was to cover the whole Earth and destroy every living thing on the face of the Earth. Then Jehovah said to Noah, "Make yourself an ark." Jehovah instructed Noah just how to make the ark. It was to be 525 feet in length, 87½ feet in breadth, and 52½ feet in height (three stories). It was to be roomy enough to house Noah and his wife, Noah's three sons and their wives, seven pairs (male and female) of every clean beast of the Earth, one pair of the beasts that were not clean, seven pairs of all the different kinds of birds in the heavens, and food enough to support all during the period of the deluge.

When the ark was completed, the Flood came. For forty days and forty nights there was a downpour of water, until every living thing on the face of the Earth, outside the ark, had been destroyed. But Noah's ark floated on the face of the waters and all those on board were safe; finally it drifted onto the top of Mount Ararat and rested there.

At the end of 150 days the waters began to recede. Noah opened the windows of the ark and sent forth a dove, to see whether the waters had been abated on the Earth, but the dove returned; she had found no place to rest. Noah waited seven days and sent forth the dove a second time. At eventide she returned bearing an olive leaf in her mouth. Then Noah knew that the waters were almost gone. He waited still another seven days and sent her forth again. She did not return, and Noah knew that she had found a home on the Earth. He removed the covering from the ark and found the Earth dry. Then he built an altar and offered a burnt offering to Jehovah. "And when the Lord smelled the pleasing odor, the Lord said in his heart, 'I will never again curse the ground because of man, for the imagination of man's heart is evil from his youth'" (Gen. 8:21).

As a token of the covenant that He would not destroy by water again, God set His "bow in the cloud" (Gen. 9:13).

"And God blessed Noah and his sons, and said to them, 'Be fruitful and multiply, and fill the earth'" (Gen. 9:1).

The allegory of Noah and the flood portrays in wonderful symbology the manner in which one of the twelve fundamental faculties of being works in unfolding perfection. The faculty of renunciation is twofold in action: it eliminates error and expands the good. The word *Noah* symbolizes the sweet rest and comfort that come after the soul has worked out in consciousness certain problems, both good and evil, and has perceived that there is an original spark of divinity in us that is indeed a very sacred, holy thing and that the expansion of this original divine spark is our spiritual development. God recognizes only the good and instructs the Adam man to open his consciousness only to good thoughts, and by the waters of denial to cleanse his consciousness of the evil.

The body is divine, and every activity in the body temple is fundamentally divine. We must know this, realize it daily, if we would make our bodies fit dwelling places for the Holy Spirit.

In the lower part of the abdomen, near the base of the spinal column, is a ganglionic nerve center which, when spiritually quickened, has power to perform a wonderful work of the kind symbolized in the story of Noah and the flood. This nerve center is symbolized by Jesus' apostle Thaddaeus; it presides over the elimination of waste from the body temple; it eliminates error thoughts from the mind and expands the good.

When working under the light of Spirit, the faculty of renunciation or elimination establishes a freedom in soul and body consciousness that gives tone and strength and elasticity to the whole person. Letting go of the old in an orderly and decisive manner, at the same time laying hold of the new, engenders a sweetness and a lightness in the whole being.

Jesus said, "If any man would come after me, let him deny himself and take up his cross and follow me" (Mt. 16:24). The self that Jesus taught must be denied is the grasping personality. It must let go of its hold upon possessive ideas before there can be harmonious activity in the eliminative center. From the invisible side of life, Spirit is constantly infusing into our being more of itself and at the same time casting out of mind and body all the waste. The forgiving love of Jesus Christ is not only a wonderful spiritual stimulant for soul and body, but it is also an important factor in the eliminative process. When the voice of Spirit within proclaims to you, "Thy sins are forgiven," it means that you have opened the way for the fulfillment of the law in you. There is a discarding of personality and an increased activity of the spiritual forces. There is an inrushing of the new and a letting go of the old. Just as the flower, unfolding its petals to the sunshine and drinking in new life and strength and beauty, exhales that which is poisonous to it, so the whole being, when the law of forgiveness is satisfied, draws new life and strength and power from the one divine source and throws off the old.

While renunciation is passive in character, it is positive and decisive in action. Our innermost thoughts determine the standard that we set up in our lives, and the whole being endeavors to measure up to this standard. The degree of intelligence that finds expression in conscious thought determines the character of the manifestation. Therefore, if we would be healthy and happy and prosperous, we must learn to do healthy, hearty, positive thinking. We must not be dominated by another's will. To let someone else do our thinking for us makes us negative, indecisive, indirect. If we try to hold on and let go at the same time, renunciation and elimination in both mind and body are weak, negative, and irregular. The negative attitude wears away the greater abilities of the soul and diffuses mental poison throughout the whole being.

Holding thoughts of unhappiness, sin, sickness, and poverty is the cause of much of the inharmony that exists today. One may tie up the bowels by holding to grasping, selfish ideas. On the other hand, a person troubled by excessive looseness of bowels can be healed by a treatment to induce courage and fearlessness. A daily study of the Twenty-Third Psalm and a meditation on it are wonderful solvents for fear.

An affirmative thought sometimes produces a congested condition throughout the body and interferes with elimination. Continued strenuous affirmations, even of Truth, will sometimes cause constipation. The remedy is to relax, to let go. The words of Truth that you have affirmed must have time to work out in the subconsciousness. We can never gain possession of the kingdom of harmony until we are free to express the wisdom and the power of Spirit as divine intelligence reveals them to us.

We are born daily and we die daily. While some error thought may stick in our minds and hold fast for a season, whenever new light is born in consciousness, the old error thought loses its grasp and falls away. This life activity is illustrated beautifully in nature—in a tree, for example. Throughout the summer months, the leaves drink in new life, which they instinctively feel is in preparation; and they store up in the trunk and branches new energy for next year's unfoldment. When autumn comes and their work is accomplished, the leaves fall off, making way for the new. But here and there an old, dead leaf holds on, refusing to give way to the blustery winds and the cutting sleet. But when spring comes, and the first tiny green shoot appears beneath its clinging hand, the old leaf loses its hold and follows its comrades.

We are making our body temples eternal dwelling places for the soul. Our goal is to bring into expression the kingdom of the heavens and to establish it within us. Consequently, we need to realize consciously that the passing away of the old and the incoming of the new are results of the outworking of the law, and that we should assist in bringing about this change. Our every experience aids in establishing more firmly our identity in

Spirit, and so gives us greater freedom and power and brings us nearer the goal of perfection—perfect health in mind and body.

For a regenerative exercise in the silence, first follow the one given in Chapter 1. Then, continuing to allow the Presence to dwell at the point designated as the great solar nerve center, realize that Jesus (the indwelling Christ in action) is standing in your midst, the one controlling, directing power, saying, "Come to me, all who labor and are heavy laden, and I will give you rest" (Mt. 11:28). As these words penetrate the soul consciousness you will realize that you are letting go of all weariness, all doubt, and all fear, and that you feel a lightness and a freedom throughout your whole being. Hold this thought: *I gladly let go of the old. My whole being expands with the new life in Christ Jesus.*

Then allow the Presence to ascend to the love center, the heart; there hold the prayer: *The forgiving love of Jesus Christ cleanses, purifies, and strengthens me.*

Dwell on this thought for some time, relaxing more and more throughout the region of the cardiac and solar plexus. During the whole time be sure that the conscious mind is fully aware of the work that is going on.

Next, allow the Presence to return to the center of renunciation, located in the bowels. Meditate upon the words: *The forgiving love of Jesus Christ cleanses, purifies, and strengthens me.*

Then let the Presence ascend to the strength center in the small of the back, and affirm: *I gladly let go of weak, worn-out thoughts in mind and body. The joy of the Lord is my strength.*

Next, let the Presence cross to the order center back of the navel, and hold the prayer: *Every function and every organ is working in perfect harmony with spiritual law. Divine order is established within me.*

Then let the Presence descend again to the center of elimination, and praise God and give thanks that His spiritual word is active throughout your whole being, with all its cleansing, discriminating, purifying power, and that you are joyously working with it.

At the conclusion allow the Presence to ascend again to the point designated as the great solar nerve center, and close by repeating the Lord's Prayer.

As in previous exercises you should be conscious continually of the light of Spirit descending from the spiritual center at the crown of the head; you should in truth be conscious of every step taken in the entire exercise.

At the close of the exercise throw the attention down into the feet and beneath the feet, also into the palms of the hands, and realize perfect poise and balance throughout your whole being.

CHAPTER 13

~~~

Life Conserver

Affirmation: *Jesus Christ is now here, raising me to His consciousness of everlasting life, and I am filled with vitalizing energy and power.*

> They may rail at this life—from the hour I began it,
> I've found it a life full of kindness and bliss;
> And, until they can show me some happier planet,
> More social and bright, I'll content me with this.
> *—Moore*

HE WHOSE CONSCIOUSNESS is spiritually quickened is content with life on this planet, because he knows that he is working out all the different phases of existence here and now. He knows that his body, his mental capacity, and his environment are all a shadowing forth of the measure and the manner in which he has contacted the inner life, the life of Spirit, and he is happy and contented in unraveling his problems. He is satisfied that there is no other place that is quite so fitting for him as his place in this world, because he has made this place for himself. The soul is always jubilant and lighthearted when it is consciously traveling the road of spiritual progression.

Potentially, life's problems are already worked

out for us, but we do not consciously know this before we come to the place where we are ready to lay hold of Truth understandingly. Without the desire for greater understanding of life, without the desire for a greater degree of life activity, we should never strive for the unfoldment of the soul. Without the inner push spurring us on to greater achievement, without the urgent desire to work out the chaos and confusion into light and joy, we should never bend our energies to the realization of the divine intelligence that reveals to us the attitude we should take in all the relations of life. Yet when we develop the ability to lay hold of understanding, we find that the spirit of the Lord has gone before and accomplished the real work for us. It is obvious therefore that life's problems consist chiefly in awakening the consciousness of the spiritual powers of being and acquiring a mental grasp of them.

But in grasping these spiritual powers we should not make hard work of it. Often metaphysicians are so bent on their spiritual demonstrations that they squeeze the joy and freedom out of life. A joyful, carefree heart is one of the most valuable assets in demonstrating health and wholeness. Exalted joy is coordinate with gratitude and praise, and it is the consciousness abounding in gratitude and praise that directly relates us to God so that we may be awakened and thrilled with the creative impulses of Divine Mind. Indeed, if a person would be a master in the realm of creative ideas, he must be free from worry and doubt and misgivings, and be filled with joyful praise and anticipation. These qualities are the magnets that draw to him new inspiration out of the superconsciousness.

Life is progress, attainment, and mastery, and every new spiritual realization makes finer and stronger and more beautiful the texture of the soul. It engenders the power to draw from the invisible the fulfillment of its highest ideals.

In biblical times we see each successive leader, with his group of associates, rising higher in consciousness than his predecessors. So in individual consciousness each step forward in spiritual growth is just a more nearly perfect blossoming of an idea drawn out of the superconsciousness by an innate desire of the soul. Abraham was great, but David was a strong spiritual leader. Yet David, with all his love and knowledge, came nowhere near measuring up to Jesus' standard of life.

Divine ideas are universal in character and recognize the unity of life among people of all nations. These ideas of life, working in and through the soul, draw to them their own from the four corners of the Earth. They attach to the individual and to the environment all the grandeur and loyalty and sublimity contained in the original idea. It is through this process that both the inner and the outer lives grow rich and full and satisfying.

In demonstrating the Christ life the first thing to overcome is inertia. In the first steps in the process of evolving, there are pitfalls and stumbling blocks of which we are not aware until we trip and fall. Unless we are open to spiritual light this may happen again and again until the downward pull has established us in an indifferent state of consciousness. Confidence dies away and inertia results. But the desire and the stir of life awaken us from our inactivity and spur us onward. It is in the working out of this state of lethargy that we develop spiritual powers that we should not otherwise feel the need of.

Therefore, no matter where you are on the ladder of life, do not be discouraged. Back of all is God's eternal plan; back of all appearances your place in the world is waiting for you, and Spirit is with you every step of the way, helping you to bring God's perfection into expression. As you struggle on for the victory, a truer understanding of life appears. As you cease to resist and learn to serve even the forces that would slay you, new strength and trust begin to stir in the heart and you are no longer at the mercy of sense consciousness, the adversary which has held you in bondage for so long.

But the redeeming process must be carried on throughout the whole being. Just as spiritual realizations now stamp their images upon us, so when we were in darkness the malformed, ill-shaped thoughts of the mortal formed their mental concepts in us, and these must now be dealt with. It is through persistent realizations of perfect life, through broadening the vision and keeping the imagination stayed on the perfect patterns of life, that the false concepts are erased and spiritual faculties are established. In your deeper meditations you have attained wonderful realizations of divine life. For instance, you have been able to take a statement such as: *The purifying power of divine life is active in me through Jesus Christ,* and to concentrate upon it until the living Truth contained in the word became so alive that it was resolved back into formless essence, in which state it was dispensed throughout the soul and body consciousness, awakening every function and organ to a greater degree of power and life.

We find however that in order to establish new states of consciousness that become abiding and reliable, in voice and word and act, they must come in touch with the faculty of conscious knowing. Just as in writing, the pen is a tool in the hand of him who is directing its movements over the paper, so the intellect is a tool of Spirit; and for any realization to become firmly established in consciousness, it must be contacted and taken possession of by this power of conscious apprehension. When this takes place, the transformation extends to the intellect itself. The spiritual idea works in the human notions that have been previously formed, and mental standards are revolutionized. Then the intellect is sharpened and polished and becomes a fit tool of Spirit.

The supreme demonstration however is gaining dominion over oneself, becoming God in expression. This is the reward of living the regenerate life. We are born of the Spirit and are delivered from the body of death. Judas represents the negative pole of life, located in the generative center, and Jesus the positive pole or spiritual center, located in the crown of the head. When the life energy is spent on the mortal plane of consciousness, then the highest form of unfoldment that can be attained is that of the psychic nature. This finally agonizes the soul until it yearningly gropes after the higher life of Spirit, which yearning opens the way to the real goal of attainment. The enigma of life, the secret of regeneration, is revealed to the consciousness through affirmations and realizations that the I AM, the son of the living God, even Christ, is within us—". . . the mystery hidden for ages and generations but now made manifest to his saints. To them God chose to make known how great among the Gentiles are the riches of the glory of this mystery, which is Christ in you, the hope of glory" (Col. 1:26-27).

Regeneration means just what the word describes—a regeneration of the soul and body through a spiritual activity of the generative organs. In regeneration the generative center is no longer allowed to waste its substance on the sense plane; by pure thinking and chaste acting, it generates an uplifting, living energy in soul and body that, when raised to the Jesus Christ purity of life, arouses all the faculties to power and ability. Then the understanding of the silent and spoken word is magnified, and with the renewed thought it comes forth in a new expression in both soul and body.

The experiences we have while passing through the throes of a new birth depend largely upon our attitude of mind toward God and toward humanity.

To be born anew under the law of love is a joy. But if we allow ourselves to be reborn in the thought that we are doing penance, that we have to lose everything for the sake of Christ, the rebirth is slow and tedious. Therefore, take your stand in regeneration with a joyful heart, knowing that God will not try you beyond what you are able to stand. Then with the thought of nonresistance as regards everybody and everything, express the positive, agreeable joy that springs from the possession of good. Then your way will be made easy.

"And let him who is thirsty come, let him who desires take the water of life without price" (Rev. 22:17).

The regenerative exercise for inducing life is of great importance. It is a longer and more intricate one than any of those given in the preceding chapters.

First begin with the exercise given in Chapter 1. Then realize that you are perfectly relaxed in mind and body, continue to allow the Presence, the Holy Spirit, to dwell at the point designated as the great solar nerve center, back of the heart and stomach, and hold this prayer: *My life is with Christ in God, and all my substance is quickened and increased.*

Feel the new life that is now quickening within you flowing out through the breast and down into the innermost part of the bowels. At the same time bear in mind that the outpouring of the new spiritual life is gently descending from the spiritual center at the crown of the head. Next, let the Presence drop down to the life organs, the generative center itself, in the lowest part of the abdomen.

Here, as in every exercise when approaching this center, think of the pure, strong, sweet life of Jesus Christ. Know that right now His regenerated life is waiting to do its perfect work in you. Realize that through the help of Jesus Christ now extended to you, every coarse impulse of soul and body is transmuted into divine purity of life and purpose. With the Presence being diffused throughout the life organs, then take up the prayer: *I am Spirit and "I am the resurrection, and the life."*

You will presently be aware of a great purifying, transmuting power beginning to do its perfect work in you. Next allow the Presence again to return to the point designated as the solar nerve center. Here take up the same thought: *I am Spirit, and "I am the resurrection, and the life."*

Next allow the Presence to ascend to the power center at the root of the tongue. At this point affirm: *All power is given unto me in mind and body.*

Then allow the Presence to ascend into the front forehead, to the understanding and the will center. Affirm: *I have a perfect understanding of life, and I am divinely guided in all my ways.*

Then let the Presence descend to the order center back of the navel. At this point realize: *The law of the Spirit of life in Christ Jesus has made me free from the law of sin and death.*

Next allow the Presence to drop to the life center and realize this prayer again: *I am Spirit, and "I am the resurrection, and the life."*

Soon you will have discovered that there is a

great regenerative work going on. Not only are the impulses of sense consciousness being transmuted into their spiritual correspondents, but the essence of the very food you have taken into the body is being refined and transmuted into a higher radiation of upbuilding energy.

And now begins the process of cooperation with the Presence, the Holy Spirit, in lifting up and distributing to all parts of the soul and body being this new life-giving force. This is done by its ascending the spinal cord, also flowing out over the thousand nerve tributaries leading from the spinal cord to every part and organ.

Continuing the exercise, allow the Presence to convey this new, refined life stuff to the base of the spinal cord; then let this all-knowing Power (with your cooperation) lift it up to a point about half the distance between the base of the spinal cord and the small of the back. Allow the Presence to dwell for several moments at this halfway station, which you will discover is a great harmonizing, equalizing center. Affirm: *The peace and harmony of the Holy Spirit in me is doing its perfect work, and I rest in confidence and joy.*

Now allow the Presence to lift up the life essence to the small of the back, the strength center. But in the lifting-up process you will become aware that the new life energy is being dispensed over the nerve wires to the innermost parts of your body as well as the outermost rim of consciousness, and that there is an ever-increasing flow.

At the strength center, the small of the back, affirm: *I am made strong and pure through the Jesus Christ life now nourishing me.*

Then let the Presence carry the life force upward until it reaches the point designated as the great solar center, where it will pour the life energy like a mighty flood into the soul consciousness, from where it will find its way into all the vital parts and organs.

This will create a new activity in both the wisdom and the love centers, and the indwelling Christ will be more and more in evidence. As the head and the heart must learn to work more and more in harmony with each other, it is well to realize that a generous supply of this renewed life energy, merged with the wisdom and love of Almightiness, is being freely dispersed through invisible channels to the front forehead and that the keen, unclouded mind of Jesus Christ is dominating your conscious thinking. The Presence will continue to lift up a generous portion of the life essence to the base of the brain, the zeal center, where it will do a mighty work. Here affirm: *I enthusiastically express the wisdom and peace of infinite life.*

Then allow the Presence to carry the new life energy over a set of motor nerves that lead from the zeal center, at the base of the brain, to the eyes, and even up into the crown of the head. Realize: *The light and the intelligence of Spirit are now being manifested in me, and I see clearly.*

Next, allow the Presence to carry the new life energy from the zeal center over a set of motor nerves to the ears. Here affirm: *My ears are open, and I hear the voice of Spirit.*

Then, following the same process, let the new energy be carried to the nose, and affirm: *The discrimination and purity of Spirit are active in me.*

Now allow the Presence to carry the life current to the mouth, the root of the tongue. Here affirm: *I am free with the freedom of Spirit.*

You will remember that at the root of the tongue and extending down into the neck is situated the throne of power. When the Presence carries the life current from the zeal center at the base of the brain, to the power center at the root of the tongue, a mighty vibration is set up that affects the whole sympathetic nervous system. You indirectly impart new life and energy to the whole digestive tract; you also strengthen and deepen your voice and revitalize your teeth.

In the Bible, you will recall, is given an account of Jesus' turning water into wine at Cana in Galilee. Metaphysically this means that when the Presence carries the new life current from the zeal center at the base of the brain, to the power center at the root of the tongue, the union (symbolized by the wedding) of the new life current with the power energy manufactures a new element, of which wine is the symbol.

With this knowledge in mind, now allow the Presence to make this union between the zeal and power centers. Affirm: *I am a new creature in Christ Jesus.*

Then quietly allow the Presence to descend to the point designated as the solar center, where you close the exercise by repeating the Lord's Prayer.

As in the previous exercises, it is absolutely necessary to be perfectly relaxed in mind and body, with the conscious mind fully aware of every step.

After the exercise is finished, throw the attention down into the feet and beneath the feet, also into the palms of the hands, and dwell at each point for some time, as it tends to keep you in perfect poise and balance.

Then go forth in this new life consciousness, expressing it through every function and organ of your whole being.

"Now as they were eating, Jesus took bread, and blessed, and broke it, and gave it to the disciples and said, 'Take, eat; this is my body.' And he took a cup, and when he had given thanks he gave it to them, saying, 'Drink of it, all of you; for this is my blood of the covenant, which is poured out for many for the forgiveness of sins.'"

—Matthew 26:26-28

Chapter 14

⟨✦⟩

Twelve-Power Exercise

The artists of old always painted their saints with a circle of light around the head, and they also painted them with a soft, warm, rose-colored glow around the heart, or with soft, rosy rays of light radiating from the heart. Let us consider if there is a metaphysical Truth back of this old practice. We believe there is. The spiritual center in the crown of the head is the throne of the Christ, the throne of the I AM. The heart itself is the seat of manifest love, which is always expressed in a warm, rosy glow of light. But it is from the I AM center in the crown of head that we draw all new inspiration, all new ideas. When they contact our consciousness, these new ideas or inspirations break forth as a soft, golden light (pure intelligence), which descends first to the seat of the conscious mind in the front forehead, and to the faith center in the pineal gland at the center of the head. Then the flow descends into the cardiac and solar nerve centers at the very center of the body, in the region of the heart and stomach, where the Christ power really begins to become manifest in substance. Often this light of Spirit (pure intelligence) not only causes the whole countenance to shine with its radiance but also surrounds

the head, and in those who live very close to Christ
the whole being is encompassed by it. While one
may feel the flow from the crown of the head to the
soles of the feet, it is in the depths of the body, in
what we term the great solar center or distributing
station, that the indwelling Christ begins to do its
great work.

Please do not get confused. The Christ throne,
the I AM center, is in the crown of the head; while
the center of the manifest Christ is the point back of
the heart and stomach that we have named the great
solar center. The apostle James wrote of the throne of
Christ: "Every good endowment and every perfect
gift is from above, coming down from the Father of
lights with whom there is no variation or shadow due
to change." In other words, the perfect pattern, or
perfect idea, which we must learn to bring into
manifestation, comes down from the *Father of lights.*
Thus we perceive that these old prophets had a true
understanding of spirituality. In the unfoldment of
the twelve powers, the most important point is
first to call forth the Christ mind, then the ingre-
dients or attributes of the Christ mind, the twelve
fundamental ideas in Divine Mind, which are faith,
strength, wisdom, love, power, imagination, understanding, will, order, zeal, renunciation, life.

As these twelve fundamental ideas begin their
work in omnipresent substance at the point designated as the solar center, where the manifest Christ
holds forth, the Lord's body begins to shape itself.
Jesus was born in Bethlehem (*Bethlehem* meaning

"house of bread") in the stable (among the animal forces). He is our Way-Shower. Just as it was necessary for Spirit in Him to penetrate the most material parts of His being, into the very animal forces, to begin the redemptive work, so it is necessary for us to do likewise.

Just as Jesus Christ was the star actor in His and His disciples' ministry here on Earth, so the indwelling Christ is the central figure in unfolding the twelve great powers in the individual. First, we set into activity the indwelling Christ mind, then gently call forth the disciples.

For the exercise in the silence, first center the attention in the crown of the head (the I AM throne) and realize that you are releasing in consciousness the idea of infinite knowing. As you truly get this realization, and as the radiations from it penetrate the soul, you will be conscious of the emanation of Spirit as pure light, pure intelligence, descending within you; you will feel it working in every cell and fiber of your body temple. As stated before, you will gradually discover that this emanation of Spirit first drops to the faith center at the center of the head and that the seat of the conscious mind, the front forehead, is illumined.

From that high vantage point, the crown of the head and front forehead, you will become aware that your whole being is suffused with this soft flow of infinite intelligence, including the very feet, even the space beneath the feet. There realize that this descending spiritual flow is contacting and tempering an earthy current steadily ascending from below. Realize that the all-knowing power of Spirit is transforming such thoughts of the race as fear, lack, war, sin, and sickness into thoughts of fearlessness, abundance, peace, justice, purity, and health.

The earthly flow, when rightly handled, will bring to you new power and ability, and will even give you a broader understanding of life in its manifest form. It will gradually ascend, permeating and penetrating the whole being in its upward course, meeting the continual outpouring from on high and at certain points in the body temple establishing centers in consciousness. But the larger portion of this renewed force goes to the seat of consciousness already designated as the great solar center at the hub of being, back of the heart and stomach.

Then from the feet and beneath the feet, follow the current to the seat of the manifest Christ, and dwell there, taking up separately and meditating on each of the twelve fundamental ideas in God-Mind—faith, strength, wisdom, love, power, imagination, understanding, will, order or law, zeal, renunciation, and life. Then, realize that twelve rays of light go forth from the great solar nerve center: one to the faith center in the pineal gland at the center of the head, another ray of light goes to the strength center in the small of the back, another to the wisdom center at the pit of the stomach, another to the love center—the heart itself, another to the power center at the root of the tongue, the next to the center of imagination located between the eyes, the next to the will and understanding centers in the front forehead, the next to the order center just back of the navel, the next to the zeal center at the base of the brain, the next to the elimination center in the lower abdominal area, and the last to the generative center in the lowest part of the abdomen. It is good for you consciously to cooperate by following these different rays of light that reach to the twelve principal centers and by holding special statements of Truth for the development of each individual center. As you accompany the Presence to the faith center, quickly affirm at this point: *I have faith in God.* Return to the center of being (the great solar nerve center) with the same affirmation. Next, go to the strength center, the small of the back, with the statement: *God is the strength of my life.* Return to the central station with the same prayer. Then ascend to the power center with the word: *I am peaceful and posed in divine power.* Return to the great central station with the same word. Then go to the imagination center with the thought: *I am created in the image and after the likeness of God.* Return to the center of being with the same thought. Follow the next ray to the understanding center with the word: *My understanding is of God.* Return with the same word to the central station. Then follow the next ray to the will center with the word: *My will is to obey God's will.* Return to the center of being with the same prayer. Next, go to the order center with the prayer: *I am one with divine order.* Return to the central station with the same affirmation. Then follow the next ray of light to the zeal center with the prayer: *I am zealous in my endeavor to work in perfect accord with infinite wisdom.* Return to the solar center with the same prayer. Next, go to the elimination center with the affirmation: *I gladly let go of the old and lay hold of the new.* Return to the central station with the same affirmation. Then follow the next ray of light to the life center with the prayer: *My life is hid with Christ in God.* Return to the great solar center with the same declaration. When approaching the life center, the lowest part of the abdomen, always first take up the thought of Jesus Christ's purity and power. At the close of the exercise allow the Presence to dwell at the central solar station in the region of the cardiac and solar plexus while you repeat the Lord's Prayer in this manner:

> Our Father who art in heaven,
> Hallowed be thy name.
> Thy kingdom come.
> Thy will be done
>   In earth, as it is in heaven.
> Give us this day our daily bread.
> And forgive us our debts,
>   As we also have forgiven our
>   debtors.
> And leave us not in temptation,
>   But deliver us from evil.
> For Thine is the kingdom,
>   and the power, and the glory,
>   for ever. Amen.

During this entire exercise the student must continue to realize that the light of Spirit from on high is descending as new inspiration, dealing in perfect order with the ascending earthly flow, and that there is perfect relaxation in mind and body. Then, realizing that the exercise is completed, behold yourself as a spiritual being, clothed in the Lord's body, firmly established in your I AM power and dominion, all the twelve faculties finding expression through the great solar station, the radiations therefrom filling the breast with new life and inspiration. With your feet planted on the firm rock of spiritual understanding, behold yourself a new creature open only to the good.

Nothing is truly ours until we express it. No new power is ours until we send it forth into the world. That which we gain in these exercises must be given forth. Remember that Jesus Christ walked and talked and lived with mankind. "And we all, with unveiled face, beholding the glory of the Lord, are being changed into his likeness from one degree of glory to another; for this comes from the Lord who is Spirit" (2 Cor. 3:18).

About the Authors

Charles Fillmore was an innovative thinker, a pioneer in metaphysical thought at a time when most religious thought in America was entirely orthodox. He was a lifelong advocate of the open, inquiring mind, and he took pride in keeping abreast of the latest scientific and educational discoveries and theories. Many years ago he wrote, "What you think today may not be the measure for your thought tomorrow"; and it seems likely that were he to compile this book today, he might use different metaphors, different scientific references, and so on.

Truth is changeless. Those who knew Charles Fillmore best believe that he would like to be able to rephrase some of his observations for today's readers, thus giving them the added effectiveness of contemporary thought. But the ideas themselves— the core of Charles Fillmore's writings—are as timeless now (and will be tomorrow) as when they were first published.

Charles Fillmore was born on an Indian reservation just outside the town of St. Cloud, Minnesota, on August 22, 1854. He made his transition on July 5, 1948, at Unity Village, Missouri, at the age of 93. To get a sense of history, when Charles was eleven, Abraham Lincoln was assassinated; when

Charles died, Harry Truman was President.

With his first wife Myrtle, Charles Fillmore founded the Unity movement and Silent Unity, the international prayer ministry that publishes *Daily Word*. Charles and Myrtle built the worldwide organization that continues their work today, Unity School of Christianity. Through Unity School's ministries of prayer, education, and publishing, millions of people around the world are finding the teachings of Truth discovered and practiced by Charles and Myrtle Fillmore.

Charles Fillmore was a spiritual pioneer whose impact has yet to be assessed. No lesser leaders than Dr. Norman Vincent Peale and Dr. Emmet Fox were profoundly influenced by him. Dr. Peale borrowed his catchphrase *positive thinking* from Charles Fillmore. Emmet Fox was so affected by Fillmore's ideas that he changed his profession. From being an engineer, he became the well-known writer and speaker.

Charles Fillmore—author, teacher, metaphysician, practical mystic, husband, father, spiritual leader, visionary—has left a legacy that continues to impact the lives of millions of people. By his fruits, he is continuously known.

Cora Fillmore was born Cora Dedrick on December 15, 1876, and came to work as secretary to Charles around 1905. Ordained a minister in 1918, she served as director of Silent Unity for a brief period and then became private secretary to both Charles and Myrtle until Myrtle's death in

October 1931. In December 1933, she became Charles' second wife when they were married at the home of Lowell Fillmore at Unity Farm. The following day they left on an extensive tour of the country to lecture on the teachings of Unity!

In 1939 Cora served on the faculty of Unity School of Christianity. She cowrote with Charles *Teach Us to Pray* and compiled two other books from the writings of Charles, *Keep a True Lent* and *Atom-Smashing Power of Mind.* She made her transition on January 29, 1955.

Unity Classic Library Series
Offers Timeless Titles of Spiritual Renewal

Every book in this series has earned the "classic" status due to its popularity, durability, and uncompromising quality. Each brings a special viewpoint and understanding of the beliefs and principles of Unity. Each book is a respected addition to any metaphysical collection.

H. EMILIE CADY
Lessons in Truth

CHARLES FILLMORE
Atom-Smashing Power
of Mind
Jesus Christ Heals
Keep a True Lent
Mysteries of Genesis
Mysteries of John
Prosperity
Talks on Truth

CHARLES AND CORA
FILLMORE
Teach Us to Pray
The Twelve Powers

LOWELL FILLMORE
The Prayer Way to Health,
Wealth, and Happiness

MYRTLE FILLMORE
How to Let God Help You

FRANCES W. FOULKS
Effectual Prayer

IMELDA SHANKLIN
What Are You?

ELIZABETH SAND
TURNER
Be Ye Transformed
Let There Be Light
Your Hope of Glory

GEORGIANA TREE WEST
Prosperity's Ten
Commandments

ERNEST C. WILSON
The Week That Changed
the World